# RADIO BOYS CRONIES

## or Bill Brown's Radio

Wayne Whipple

S. F. Aaron

1st WORLD
LIBRARY
Literary Society

# Radio Boys Cronies

## Wayne Whipple and S. F. Aaron

© 1st World Library, 2006
PO Box 2211
Fairfield, IA 52556
www.1stworldlibrary.com
First Edition

LCCN: 2006935361

Softcover ISBN: 1-4218-2506-6
Hardcover ISBN: 1-4218-2406-X
eBook ISBN: 1-4218-2606-2

Purchase "*Radio Boys Cronies*"
as a traditional bound book at:
www.1stWorldLibrary.com/purchase.asp?ISBN=1-4218-2506-6

1st World Library is a literary, educational organization
dedicated to:

- Creating a free internet library of downloadable ebooks

- Hosting writing competitions and offering book
publishing scholarships.

Interested in more 1st World Library books?
contact: literacy@1stworldlibrary.com
Check us out at: www.1stworldlibrary.com

# 1ˢᵗ World Library Literary Society

## Giving Back to the World

"If you want to work on the core problem, it's early school literacy."

**- James Barksdale, former CEO of Netscape**

"No skill is more crucial to the future of a child, or to a democratic and prosperous society, than literacy."

**- Los Angeles Times**

Literacy... means far more than learning how to read and write... The aim is to transmit... knowledge and promote social participation."

**- UNESCO**

"Literacy is not a luxury, it is a right and a responsibility. If our world is to meet the challenges of the twenty-first century we must harness the energy and creativity of all our citizens."

**- President Bill Clinton**

"Parents should be encouraged to read to their children, and teachers should be equipped with all available techniques for teaching literacy, so the varying needs and capacities of individual kids can be taken into account."

**- Hugh Mackay**

# CHAPTER I

## THE CRONIES

"Come along, Bill; we'll have to get there, or we won't hear the first of it. Mr. Gray said it would begin promptly at three."

"I'm doing my best, Gus. This crutch -"

"I know. Climb aboard, old scout, and we'll go along faster." The first speaker, a lad of fifteen, large for his age, fair-haired, though as brown as a berry and athletic in all his easy, deliberate yet energetic movements, turned to the one he had called Bill, a boy of about his own age, or a little older, but altogether opposite in appearance, for he was undersized, dark-haired, black-eyed, and though a life-long cripple with a twisted knee, as quick and nervous in action as the limitations of his physical strength and his ever-present crutch permitted.

In another moment, despite the protests of generous consideration for his chum's strenuous offer, William Brown was heaved up on the broad back of Augustus Grier and the two cronies thus progressed quite rapidly for a full quarter of a mile through the residential section of Fairview. Not until the pair arrived at the entrance of one of the outlying cottages did husky Gus cease to be the beast of burden, though he was greatly tempted to turn into a charging war horse when one of a group of urchins on a street corner shouted:

"Look at the monkey on a mule!"

Gus cared nothing for taunts and slurs against himself, but he deeply resented any suggestion of insult aimed at his crippled friend. However, although Bill could not defend his reputation with his fists, a method which most appealed to Gus, the lame boy had often proved that he had a native wit and a tongue that could give as good as was ever given him.

"Here we are, Gus, and how can I ever get square with you?" Bill said, his crutch and loot thumping the steps as the boys gained the doorway.

In answer to the bell, a sweet-faced lady opened the door, greeted the boys by name and ushered them into a book-lined study where already several other boys and girls of about the same age were gathered about their school teacher.

Professor James B. Gray, although this was vacation time, was the sort of man who got real and continued pleasure out of instruction, especially concerning his hobbies. Thus his advanced classes, here represented, had come into much additional knowledge regarding the microscope and the stereopticon and had also greatly enjoyed the Professor's moving-picture apparatus devoted to serious subjects. The latest wonder, and one worthy of intense interest, was a newly installed radio receiver.

"Come in, come in, David and Jonathan, - I mean William and Augustus!" greeted Professor Gray. "Find chairs, boys. I'm glad you've come. Now, then, exactly in nine minutes the lecture starts and it will interest you. The announcement, as sent out yesterday, makes the subject the life and labors of the great scientist and inventor, Thomas Alva Edison, and it begins with his boyhood. Don't you think that a fitting subject upon an occasion where electricity is the chief factor? But before the time is up, let me say a few words concerning our little boxed instrument here, out of which will come the words we hope to hear. Some of you, I think, have become pretty familiar with this subject, but for those who have not given much attention to radio, I will briefly outline the principles upon which these sounds we shall hear are made possible.

"It would seem that our earth and atmosphere," continued the Professor, "and all of the universe, probably, is surcharged with electrical energy that may be readily set in motion through the mechanical vibrations of a sensitive diaphragm much as when one speaks into a telephone. This motion is transmitted in waves of varying intensity and frequency which are sent into space by the mechanism of the broadcasting station, which consists of a sound conducting apparatus induced by strong electrical currents from generators or batteries and extensive aerial or antennas wires high in the air. Thus sound is converted into waves, and the receiving station, as you see here, with its aerial on the roof, its detector, its 'phone and its tuner, gets these waves and turns them again into sound. That is the outline of the thing, which you will understand better 'after' than 'before using.'

"The technical construction of the radio receiving set is neither difficult nor expensive; it is described fully in several books on the subject and I shall be glad to give any of you hints on the making and the operation of a receiving set. The 'phone receivers and the crystal detector will have to be purchased as well as some of the accessories, such as the copper wire, pulleys, battery, switches, binding posts, the buzzer tester and so forth. With proper tools and much ingenuity some of these appliances may be home-made.

"The making of the tuner, the wiring, the aerial and the assembling are all technicalities that may be mastered by a careful study of the subject and the result will be a simple and inexpensive set having a limited range. With more highly perfected appliances, as a vacuum, or audion tube, and an aerial elevated from sixty to over a hundred feet, you may receive radio energy thousands of miles away.

"Now, this talk we are about to hear comes to us from the broadcasting station WUK at Wilmerding, a distance of three hundred miles, and this outfit of mine is such as to get the words loudly and clearly enough to be audible through a horn. The talks are in series; there have been three on modern poets, two on the history of great railroad systems and now this will be the first of several on great inventors, beginning with Edison, in four parts. The next will be on Friday and I want you all to be here. Time is up; there will be a preliminary-ah, there it is: a cornet solo by Drake."

Wayne Whipple and S. F. Aaron

# CHAPTER II

## AN UNUSUAL LAD

Professor Gray turned to the box and began moving the metal switch arms back and forth, thus tuning in more perfectly as indicated by the increased and clearer sound and the absence of interference from other broadcasting stations, noticed at first by a low buzzing. In a moment the music came clear and sweet, the stirring tune of "America." When the sound of the cornet ceased, there followed this announcement:

"My subject is the early life of Thomas Alva Edison."

Everyone settled down most contentedly and Gus saw Bill hug himself in anticipatory pleasure; the lame boy had always been a staunch admirer of the great inventor. There was no need of calling anyone's attention to the necessity for keeping quiet. Out of the big horn, as out of a phonograph, came the deliberate and carefully enunciated words:

"It has been said that 'the boy is father to the man.' That may be worthy of general belief; at least evidences of it are to be found in the boyhood of him we delight to speak of as one of the first citizens of our country and probably the greatest scientific discoverer of all time. The boyhood of this remarkable man was almost as remarkable as his manhood; it was full of incidents showing the tendencies that afterward contributed to true greatness in the chosen field of endeavor of a mind bent upon experiment, discovery and invention.

"Thomas Alva Edison was born in Milan, Ohio, in the year 1847. The precise date, even to Mr. Edison, seems somewhat doubtful.

"He was a frail little chap, with an older brother and sister. But he was active enough to have several narrow escapes from death. He wouldn't have been a real boy if he hadn't fallen into the canal and barely escaped drowning at least once.

"Then while he was a little bit of a fellow, climbing and prowling around a grain elevator beside the canal, he fell into the wheat bin and was nearly smothered to death.

"Once he held a skate strap for another boy to cut off with a big ax and the lad sliced off the end of the fingers holding it!

"Another time the small Edison boy was investigating a bumblebee's nest in a field close to the fence. He was so interested in watching the bees that he didn't notice a cross old ram till it had butted in and sent him sprawling. Although he was then 'between two fires,' the little lad was quick-witted enough to jump up and climb the fence just in time to escape a second attack from the ugly old beast. From a safe place he watched the bees and the ram with keen concern. But Edison says his mother used up a lot of arnica on his small frame after this double encounter. The little lad early learned to observe that 'It's a great life if you don't weaken!'

"Mr. Edison tells this story about himself:

"'Even as a small boy, before we moved away from Milan, I used to try to make experiments. Once I built a fire in a barn. I remember how startled I was to see how fast a fire spreads in such a place. Almost before I knew it the barn was in flames and I barely escaped with my life.

"The neighbors thought I ought to be disciplined and made an example of. My mortified parents consented and I was publicly whipped in the village square. I suppose it was a good lesson to me and made the neighbors feel easier. But I think seeing that barn burning down made me feel worse than the whipping, - though I felt I deserved that, too.'

"The Edisons moved to Port Huron, Michigan, and lived a little way out of the town on the St. Clair river, where it flows out of Lake Huron. The house was in an orchard, but within easy walking distance of the town. There was no compulsory school law in those days and young Edison did not attend school, but his mother taught him all she could. She was a good teacher - she had taught school before she was married - but even she could not be answering questions all the time. There was a public library in town, so the boy spent a good deal of his time there. He would have liked to read all the books in the library - but he started in on a cyclopedia. He thought because there was 'something about everything' in that, he'd know all there was to know if he read it through. But he soon found question after question to ask that the cyclopedia did not answer. Some of the books he took home to read.

"Mr. Edison, the boy's father, had built a wooden tower that permitted a beautiful view of the town, River St. Clair and Lake Huron; one could see miles around in Michigan and over into Canada. Mr. Edison charged ten cents a head to go up and get the view on top of this tower. Very few people came, so the tower was not a great success. But the boy went up there to read, not caring so much for the view as to be alone.

"Young Edison read all he could find about electricity. That always fascinated him. But the father seemed to have a hard time making a living and Al, as they called the boy, went to work. He began selling newspapers in Port Huron, but there was not much in that, so he got a chance to sell on the seven o'clock train for Detroit. He applied at the Grand Trunk offices for the job and made his arrangements before he told any one. He had to be at the station at 6:30 A.M. and have his stock all ready before the train started, which compelled him to leave home at six. The train was a local with only three cars

- baggage, smoking and passenger. The baggage car was partitioned off into three compartments. One of these was never used, so Al was allowed to take that for his papers to which he added fruits, candies and other wares.

"The run down to Detroit took over three hours. His train did not start back till 4:30 in the afternoon, so the lad had about six hours in the big city. He took all the time he needed to buy stock to sell on the train and to eat his lunch. This left him several hours for reading in the Detroit public library, where he found more books on the subjects he liked, more answers to appease his never abating curiosity."

# CHAPTER III

## GETTING THE MONEY-MAKING HABIT

"Those were the anxious days of the Civil War," the lecturer continued, "and every-one was worked up to a high pitch of excitement most of the time. When it was rumored that a battle had been fought the newspapers sold 'like hot cakes.' Any other boy would have been satisfied if he could supply as many papers as people wanted and let it go at that. But that was not the way with young Edison. He was not content with hoping for an opportunity. He made his opportunity.

"In spite of his getting into trouble so often, Al was a most likable lad, and a real boy, - earnest, honest and industrious. He had a big stock of horse sense and a great fund of humor. Though his life seemed to be 'all work and no play,' he took great pleasure in his work. In the course of his daily routine at Detroit, he could hardly help making friends on the *Free Press*, the greatest newspaper there. In this he resembled that other great inventor, also a great worker as a boy - Benjamin Franklin.

"Young Edison had a friend up in the printing office who let him see proofs from the edition being set up, so that he kept posted as to what was to be in the paper before it came off the press. After the *Free Press* came out, he had to get an armful and hustle for his train. In this shrewd way the train-boy was better off than 'he who runs may read,' for he *had* read, and could *shout* while running: 'All about the big battle!' So he sold his papers in short order. He had learned to estimate ahead how many papers the news of a battle ought to sell, and so he stocked up well beforehand. One day he saw in the advance proofs a harrowing account of the great two-days' battle of Shiloh. He grasped not only the news value but also the strategic importance of that victory.

"Running down to the telegraph office at the Grand Trunk Station in Detroit, he told the operator all about it. Edison has told us himself about the offer he made that telegrapher:

"'If you will wire to every station on my run and get the station master to chalk up on the blackboard out on the station platform that there has been a big battle, with thousands killed and wounded, I'll give you *Harper's Weekly* free for six months!'

"The operator agreed and that Edison boy tore back to the *Free Press* office.

"'I want a thousand papers!' he gasped. 'Pay you to-morrow!' This was more than three times as many as he had taken out before, so the clerk refused to trust him.

"'Where's Mr. Storey?' demanded the lad. The clerk snickered as he jerked his head toward where the managing editor was talking with a 'big' man from out of town. Young Edison was forced to break in, but the editor noticed how anxious and business-like he was. When the boy had told him what he wanted, the great newspaper man scribbled a few words on a scrap of paper and handed it down to him, saying:

"'Here, take this. Wish you good luck!'

"Al handed the clerk the order and got his thousand papers at once. He hired another 'newsie' to help him down to the station with them. Long after this, he told the rest of the story:

"'At Utica, the first station, twelve miles out of Detroit, I usually sold two papers at five cents each. As we came up I put my head out and thought I saw an excursion party. The people caught sight of me and commenced to shout. Then it began to occur to me that they wanted papers. I rushed back into the car, grabbed an armful, and sold forty there.

"'Mt. Clemens was the next stop. When that station came in sight, I thought there was a riot. The platform was crowded with a howling mob, and I realized that they were after news of Shiloh, so I raised the price to ten cents, and sold a hundred and fifty where I never had got rid of more than a dozen.

"'At other stations these scenes were repeated, but the climax came when we got to Port Huron. I had to jump off the train about a quarter of a mile from the station which was situated out of town. I had paid a big Dutch boy to haul several loads of sand to that point, and the engineers knew I was going to jump so they slowed down a bit. Still, I was quite an expert on the jump. I heaved off my bundle of papers and landed all right. As usual, the Dutch boy met me and we carried the rest of the papers toward the town.

"'We had hardly got half way when we met a crowd hurrying toward the station. I thought I knew what they were after, so I stopped in front of a church where a prayer-meeting was just closing. I raised the price to twenty-five cents and began taking in a young fortune.

"'Almost at the same moment the meeting closed and the people came rushing out. The way the coin materialized made me think the deacons had forgotten to pass the plate in that meeting!'

"In those days they commonly called trainboys 'Candy Butchers'; the terms 'Newsies' and 'Peanuts' may have been used then also but were not so common. They are not so common on trains nowadays, except in the West and South, but formerly they were even more of an institution than the water cooler or the old-fashioned winter stove. The station-shouting brakemen were no more familiar or comforting to weary passengers than the 'candy butchers' and their welcome stock."

# CHAPTER IV

## *Paul Pry* ON WHEELS

"With all he had to do, young Edison found that he had time on his hands which he might yet put to good use. One would think being 'candy butcher' and newsboy from 6 A.M. to 9 P.M., and making from $10.00 to $12.00 a day might satisfy the boy's cravings. But contentment wasn't one of Al Edison's numerous virtues.

"He did not know it, but he was following the footsteps of that other great American inventor, Benjamin Franklin, as a printer, editor, proprietor and publisher. In one of the stores where he stocked up with books, magazines and stationery for his train, there was an old printing press which the dealer, Mr. Roys, had taken for a debt. Mr. Roys once told the little story of that press:

"'Young Edison, who was a good boy and a favorite of mine, bought goods of me and had the run of the store. He saw the press, and I suppose he thought at once that he would publish a paper himself, for he could catch onto a new idea like lightning. He got me to show him how it worked, and finally bought it for a small sum.'

"From his printer friends on the *Free Press* he bought some old type. Watching the compositors at work, he learned to set type and make up the forms, so within two weeks after purchasing the press he brought out the first number of *The Weekly Herald*

- the first paper ever written, set up, proof-read, printed, published and sold (besides all his other work) on a local train - and this by a boy of fourteen!

"Of course, it had to be a sort of local paper, giving train and station gossip with sage remarks and 'preachments' from the boy's standpoint. It sold for three cents a copy, or eight cents a month to regular customers. Its biggest 'sworn circulation' was 700 copies, of which about 500 were *bona fide* subscriptions, and the rest 'news-stand sales.'

"The great English engineer, Robert Stephenson, grandson of the inventor and improver of the locomotive, is said to have ordered a thousand copies to be distributed on railways all over the world to show what an American newsboy could do.

"Even the *London Times*, known for generations as '*The Thunderer*,' and long considered the greatest newspaper in both hemispheres, quoted from *The Weekly Herald*, as the only paper of its kind in the world. Young Edison's news venture was a financial success, for it added $45.00 a month to his already large income.

"But *Paul Pry* came to grief because he tried to be funny in disclosing the secret motives of certain persons. People differ widely in their notions about fun. In a local paper, too, some one's feelin's are likely to get 'lacerated!' This was the case with a six-foot subscriber to the paper which was published then under Al Edison's pen name of 'Paul Pry.' One day the juvenile editor happened to meet his huge and wrathy reader too near the St. Clair river. Whereupon the subscriber took the editor by his collar and waistband and heaved him, neck and crop, into the river. Edison swam to shore, wet, but otherwise undisturbed, discontinued the publication of *Paul Pry*, and bade good-by to journalism forever!

"While young Edison was wading through such mammoth works as Sears's *History of the World*, Burton's *Anatomy of Melancholy*, and the *Dictionary of Sciences* (and had begun to

Wayne Whipple and S. F. Aaron

wrestle desperately with Newton's *Principia*!) he was showing a rare passion for chemistry. He 'annexed' the cellar for a laboratory. His mother said she counted, at one time, no less than two hundred bottles of chemicals, all shrewdly marked POISON, so that no one but himself would dare to touch them. Before long the lad took up so much room in his mother's cellar with his 'mess,' as she called it, that she told him to take it out, 'bag and baggage.'

"He once stated that his great desire to make money was largely because he needed the cash to buy materials for experiments. Therefore, in this emergency, he took keen pleasure in buying all the chemicals, appliances and apparatus he wished, and installing them in his real 'bag and baggage' car. As the railroad authorities had allowed him to set up a printing press, in addition to his miscellaneous stock in trade, why should he not have his laboratory there also? So his stock of batteries, chemicals and other 'calamity' grew apace.

"One day, after several weeks of happiness in his moving laboratory, he was 'dead to the world' in an experiment. Suddenly the car gave a lurch and jolted the bottle of phosphorus off its shelf. It broke, flamed up, set fire to the floor and endangered the whole train. While the boy was frantically fighting the fire, the Scotch conductor, red-headed and wrathy, rushed in and helped him to put it out.

"By this time they were stopping at Mt. Clemens, where the indignant Scotchman boxed the boy's ears and put him out also. Then the man threw the lad's bottles, apparatus and batteries after him, as if they were unloading a carload of freight there.

"These blows on his ears were the cause of the inventor's life-long deafness. But there never was a gamer sport than Thomas A. Edison. Once, long after this, he saw the labor of years and the outlay of at least two million dollars at the seashore washed away in a single night by a sudden storm. He only laughed and said that was 'spilt milk, not worth crying over.'

Disappointments of that sort were 'the fortunes of war' or 'all for the best' to him. The injury so unjustly inflicted on him by that irate conductor was not a defect to him. Many years afterwards he said:

"'This deafness has been of great advantage to me in various ways. When in a telegraph office I could hear only the instrument directly on the table at which I sat, and, unlike the other operators, I was not bothered by the other instruments.

"'Again, in experimenting on the telephone, I had to improve the transmitter so that I could hear it. This made the telephone commercial, as the magneto telephone receiver of Bell was too weak to be used as a transmitter commercially.'

"It was the same with the phonograph. The great defect of that instrument was the rendering of the overtones in music and the hissing consonants in speech. Edison worked over one year, twenty hours a day, Sundays and all, to get the word 'specie' perfectly recorded and reproduced on the phonograph. When this was done, he knew that everything else could be done, - which was a fact.

"'Again,' Edison resumed, 'my nerves have been preserved intact. Broadway is as quiet to me as a country village is to a person with normal hearing.'"

The talk suddenly ceased. Then another voice announced from out of the horn: "The second installment of the lectures on Edison will be given at 3 P.M. next Friday. We will now hear a concert by Wayple's band."

# CHAPTER V

## OPINIONS

The boys and girls filed out, after most of them had expressed appreciation of Professor Gray's interest in their enjoyment, and on the street a lively discussion started. Terry Watkins was laughing derisively at some remark of Cora Siebold, who, arm in arm with her chum "Dot" Myers, had paused long enough to fire a broadside at him.

"Why don't some of you smarties who talk so much about the wonderful things you can do make yourselves receiving sets! Too lazy? Baseball and swimming and loafing around are all you think about. But leave it to the girls; Dot and I are going to tackle one."

"What? You two? Won't it be a mess? Bet you can't hear yourselves think on it. Girls building a radio! Ho, ho, ho!"

"Bet there'll be a looking-glass in it somewhere," laughed Ted Bissell.

"Well, we aren't planning to ask advice from either of you," Cora said.

"No, and it would be worth very little if you got any," Bill Brown offered, as he and Gus, who had been detained a moment by Professor Gray, joined the loitering group.

"Thanks, Mr. Brown," said Dot, half shyly.

"Who asked you for your two cents' worth?" Terry demanded.

"I'm donating it, to your service. Go and do something yourself before you make fun of others," Bill said.

"That's right, too, Billy. Terry can't drive a carpet tack, nor draw a straight line with a ruler." Ted was always in a bantering mood and eager for a laugh at anybody. "I'll bet Cora's radio will radiate royally and right. You going to make one - you and Gus?"

"I guess we can't afford it," Bill replied quickly. "We're both going to work in the mill next Monday. Long hours and steady, and not too much pay, either. But we need the money; eh, Gus?"

"We do," agreed Gus, smiling.

Bill's countenance was altogether rueful. Life had not been very kind to him and he very naturally longed for some opportunity to dodge continued hardship. He wished that he might, like the boy Edison, make opportunity, but that sounded more plausible in lectures than in real life. He was moodily silent now, while the others engaged in a spirited discussion started by Dot's saying kindly:

"Well, lots of boys and girls have to work and they often are the better for it. Edison did - and was."

"Oh, I guess he could have been just as great, or greater if he hadn't worked," remarked Terry sententiously. "It isn't only poor boys that amount to -'"

"Mostly," said Bill.

"Oh, of course, *you'd* say that. We'll charge your attitude up to envy."

"When I size up some of the rich men's sons I know, I'm rather glad I'm poor," said Bill, "and I would rather make a thousand dollars all by my own efforts than inherit ten thousand."

"I guess you'd take what you could get," Terry offered, and Bill was quick to reply:

"We know there'll be a lot coming to you and it will be interesting to know what you'll do with it and how long you'll have it."

"He will never add anything to it," said Ted, who also was the son of wealth, but not in the least snobbish. The others all laughed at this and Terry turned away angrily.

Bill, further inspired by what he deemed an unfair reference to Edison, began to wax eloquent to the others concerning his hero.

"I don't believe Edison would have amounted to half as much as he has if he hadn't had the hard knocks that a poor fellow always gets. Terry makes me tired with his high and mighty -"

"Oh, don't you mind him!" said Cora.

"You've read a lot about Edison, haven't you, Bill?" asked Dot, knowing that the lame boy possessed a hero worshiper's admiration for the wizard of electricity and an overmastering desire to emulate the great inventor. The girl sat down on the grassy bank, pulled Cora down beside her and in her gentle, kindly way, continued to draw Bill out. "When only quite a little fellow he had become a great reader, the lecturer said."

"I should say he was a reader!" Bill declared. "Why, when he was eleven years old he had read Hume's History of England all through and -"

"Understood about a quarter of it, I reckon," laughed Ted.

"Understood more than you think," Bill retorted. "He did more in that library than just read an old encyclopedia; he got every book off the shelves, one after the other, and dipped into them all, but of course, some didn't interest him. He read a lot on 'most every subject; mostly about science and chemistry and engineering and mechanics, but a lot also on law and even moral philosophy and what you call it? oh - ethics - and all that sort of thing. He had to read to find out things; there seemed to be no one who could tell him the half that he wanted to know, and I guess a lot of people got pretty tired of having him ask so many questions they couldn't answer. And when they would say, 'I don't know,' he'd get mad and yell: '*Why* don't you know?'"

"Hume's history, - why, we have that at home, in ten volumes. If he got outside of all of that he was going some!" declared Ted.

"Well, he did, and all of Gibbon's Decline and Fall of the Roman Empire, too."

"Holy cats! What stopped him?" Ted queried.

"He didn't stop - never stopped. But he had to earn his living - didn't he? He couldn't read all the books and find out about everything right off. But you bet he found out a lot, and he believes that after a fellow gets some rudiments of education he can learn more by studying in his own way and experimenting than by just learning by rote and rule. Maybe he's not altogether right about that, for education is mighty fine and I'd like to go to a technical school; Gus and I both are aiming for that, but we're going to read and study a lot our own way, too, and experiment; aren't we, Gus? Nobody can throw Edison's ideas down when they stop to think how much he knows and what he's done."

"He certainly has accomplished a great deal," the usually reticent Gus offered.

"And yet he seems to be very modest about it," was Cora's contribution.

"Of course, he is; every man who does really big things is never conceited," declared Bill.

"Oh, I don't know. How about Napoleon?" queried Dot.

"Napoleon? All he ever did was to get up a big army and kill people and grab a government. He had brains, of course, but he didn't put them to much real use, except for his own glory. You can't put Napoleon in the same class with Edison."

"Oh, Billy, you can't say that, can you?"

"I have said it and I'll back it up. Look how Edison has given billions of people pleasure and comfort and helped trade and commerce. Nobody could do more than that. War and fighting and being a king, - that's nothing but selfishness! Some day people will build the largest monuments to folks who have done big things for humanity, - not to generals and kings. Just knowing how to scrap isn't much good. I've got more respect for Professor Gray than I have for the champion prize fighter. You can't -"

"Maybe if you knew how to use your fists, you wouldn't talk that way; eh, Gus?" queried Ted.

"Well, I don't know but I think Bill is right. It's nice to know how to scrap if scrapping has to be done, but it shouldn't ever have to be done, - between nations, anyway." This was a long speech for Gus, but evidently he meant it.

Bill continued:

"Talking about Edison when he was a boy: he wasn't afraid of work, either. He got up at about five, got back to supper at nine, or later, and maybe that wasn't some day! But he made from $12 to $20 a day profits, for it was Civil War times and everything was high."

"I think I'd work pretty hard for that much," said Gus.

"I reckon," remarked Ted, "that he had a pretty good reason to say that successful genius is one per cent. inspiration and ninety-nine per cent. perspiration."

"But I guess that's only partly right and partly modesty," declared Bill. "There must have been a whole lot more than fifty per cent, inspiration at work to do what he has done. But he is too busy to go around blowing his own horn, even from a talking-machine record."

"He doesn't need to do any blowing when you're around," Ted offered.

Bill laughed outright at that and there seemed nothing further to be said. The girls decided to go on, Ted walked up the street with them, and Gus and his lame companion turned in the opposite direction toward the less opulent section of the town. There were chores to do at home and Gus often lent a hand to help his father who was the town carpenter. Bill, the only son of a widow whose small means were hardly adequate for the needs of herself and boy, did all he could to lessen the daily pinch.

# CHAPTER VI

## THE BOYHOOD OF A GENIUS

The class had assembled again in Professor Gray's study and all were eager to hear the second talk on Edison. There was a delay of many minutes past the hour stated, but the anticipation was such that the time was hardly noticed. During the interim, Professor Gray came to where Bill and Gus sat.

"I hear that you boys intend to go to work in the mills next week," he said. "Well, now, I have some news and a proposition, so do not be disappointed if the beginning sounds discouraging. In the first place I saw Mr. Deering, superintendent of the mills, again and he told me that while he would make good his promise to take you on, there would hardly be more than a few weeks' work. Orders are scarce and they expect to lay off men in August, though there is likely to be a resumption of business in the early fall when you are getting back into school work. So wouldn't it be better to forego the mill work, - there goes the announcement! I'll talk with you before you leave."

"But we need the money; don't we, Gus?"

"We do," said Gus.

"I wonder if the Professor thinks we're millionaires." Bill was plainly disappointed.

"Oh, well, he didn't finish what he was saying to us. Let's listen to the weather report," demanded Gus, ever optimistic and joyful.

The words came clearer than ever out of that wonderful horn. There was to be rain that afternoon - local thunderstorms, followed by clearing and cooler. On the morrow it would be cloudy and unsettled.

Bill felt as though that prediction suited his mental state! Gus was never the kind to worry; he sat smiling at the horn and he received with added pleasure the music of a band which followed. And then came the second talk on the boyhood of the master of invention.

"It has been said," spouted the horn, "that high mental characteristics are accompanied by heroic traits. Whether true or not generally, it was demonstrated in young Edison and it governed his learning telegraphy and the manner thereof. The story is told by the telegraph operator at Mt. Clemens, where the red-headed conductor threw the train boy and his laboratory off the train.

"'Young Edison,' says the station agent, 'had endeared himself to the station agents, operators and their families all along the line. As the mixed train did the way-freight work and the switching at Mt. Clemens, it usually consumed not less than thirty minutes, during which time Al would play with my little two-and-a-half-year old son, Jimmy.

"'It was at 9:30 on a lovely summer morning. The train had arrived, leaving its passenger coach and baggage car standing on the main track at the north end of the station platform, the pin between the baggage and the first box car having been pulled out. There were about a dozen freight cars, which had pulled ahead and backed in upon the freight-house siding. The train men had taken out a box car and pushed it with force enough to reach the baggage car without a brakeman controlling it.

"'At this moment Al turned and saw little Jimmy on the main track, throwing pebbles over his head in the sunshine, all unconscious of danger. Dashing his papers and cap on the platform he plunged to the rescue.

"'The train baggage man was the only eyewitness. He told me that when he saw Al jump toward Jimmy he thought sure both boys would be crushed. Seizing Jimmy in his arms just as the box car was about to strike them, young Edison threw himself off the track. There wasn't a tenth of a second to lose. By this instinctive act he saved his own life, for if he had thrown the little chap first and then himself, he would have been crushed under the wheels.

"'As it was, the front wheel struck the heel of the newsboy's boot and he and Jimmy fell, face downward on the sharp, fresh-gravel ballast so hard that they were both bleeding and the baggage man thought sure the wheel had gone over them. To his surprise their injuries proved to be only skin deep.

"'I was in the ticket office when I heard the shriek and ran out in time to see the train hands carrying the two boys to the platform. My first thought was: 'How can I, a poor man, reward the dear lad for risking his life to save my child's?' Then it came to me, 'I can teach him telegraphy.' When I offered to do this, he smiled and said, 'I'd like to learn,' and learn he did. I never saw any one pick it up so fast. It was a sort of second nature with him. After the conductor treated him so badly, throwing off his apparatus, boxing his ears and making him hard of hearing, Al seemed to lose his interest in his business as train boy.

"'Some days Al would stop at my station at half past nine in the morning and stay all day while the train went on to Detroit and returned to Mt. Clemens in the evening. The train baggage man who saw Al rescue Jimmy would get the papers in Detroit and bring them up to Mt. Clemens for him. During these long hours the Edison boy made rapid progress in learning. And every day he made the most of the half hour or more of practice he had while the train stopped at Mt. Clemens each way.

"'At the end of a couple of weeks I missed him for several days. Next time he dropped off he showed me a set of telegraph instruments he had made in a gunshop in Detroit, where the stationer who had sold him goods had told the owner of the machine shop the story of the printing press.'

"The first place young Edison worked after he was graduated from the Mt. Clemens private school of telegraphy was in Port Huron, his home town. Here he had too many boy friends to let him keep on the job as a youthful telegrapher should. Besides, he had a laboratory in his home and found it too fascinating to take enough sleep. Between too much side work and mischief, young Edison sometimes found himself in trouble. Some of his escapades he has described to his friend and assistant, William H. Meadowcroft.

"'About every night we could hear the soldiers stationed at Fort Gratiot. One would call out: "Corporal of Guard Number One!" This was repeated from one sentry to another till it reached the barracks and "No. 1" came out to see what was wanted. The Dutch boy (who used to help me with the papers) and I thought we would try our hand in military matters.

"'So one dark night I called, "Corporal of the Guard Number One!" The second sentry, thinking it had come from the man stationed at the end, repeated this, and the words went down the line as usual. This reached Corporal Number One, and brought him back to our end only to find out that he had been tricked by someone.

"'We did this three times, but on the third night they were watching. They caught the Dutch boy and locked him up in the fort. Several soldiers chased me home. I ran down cellar where there were two barrels of potatoes and a third which was almost empty. I dumped the contents of three barrels into two, sat down, pulled the empty barrel over my head, bottom upwards. The soldiers woke my father, and they all came hunting for me with lanterns and candles.

"'The corporal was perfectly sure I had come down cellar. He couldn't see how I had got away, and asked father if there wasn't a secret place for me to hide in the cellar. When father said "No," he exclaimed, "Well, that's very strange!"

"'You can understand how glad I was when they left, for I was in a cramped position, and as there had been rotten potatoes in that barrel, I was beginning to feel sick.

"'The next morning father found me in bed and gave me a good switching on my legs - the only whipping I ever received from him, though mother kept behind the old clock a switch which had the bark well worn off! My mother's ideas differed somewhat from mine, most of all when I mussed up the house with my experiments.

"'The Dutch boy was released the next morning.'

"Another escapade described by Edison was pulled off on the Canada side of the St. Clair, in Port Sarnia, opposite Port Huron.

"'In 1860 the Prince of Wales (afterward King Edward) visited Canada. Nearly every lad in Port Huron, including myself, went over to Sarnia to see the celebration. The town was profusely draped in flags - there were arches over some streets - and carpets were laid on the crossings for the prince to walk on.

"'A stand was built where the prince was to be received by the mayor. Seeing all these arrangements raised my idea of the prince very high. But when he finally came I mistook the Duke of Newcastle for Albert Edward. The duke was a very fine-looking man. When I discovered my mistake - the Prince of Wales being a mere stripling - I was so disappointed that I couldn't help mentioning the fact. Then several of us American boys expressed our belief that a prince wasn't much after all! One boy got well whipped for this and there was a free-for-all fight. The Canucks attacked the Yankee boys and, as they greatly outnumbered us, we were all badly licked and I got a black eye. This always prejudiced me against that kind of ceremonial and folly.'"

# CHAPTER VII

## THE MAKING OF AN INVENTOR

"It was during the time young Edison was employed at Port Huron," the radio continued, "that the cable under River St. Clair between that city and Port Sarnia was severed by an ice jam. The river at that point is three quarters of a mile wide. Navigation was suspended and the ice had broken up so that the stream could not be crossed on foot nor could the broken cable lying in the bed of the river be mended.

"The ingenious young telegrapher suggested signaling Sarnia by giving, with the whistle of a locomotive, the dot-and-dash letters of the Morse telegraph code. Or course, this strange whistling caused considerable wonderment on the Canada side until a shrewd operator recognized the long-and-short telegraph letters, and communication was at once established - important messages being transmitted by steam whistles - a gigantic system of broadcasting. This was a simple way out of a sublime difficulty involving the affairs of two great peoples.

"But the too-enterprising operator had started so much trouble for himself that he decided to find employment where his mind would not be distracted from his job or tempted away from working out his chemical and electrical experiments. Because of these he preferred the position of night operator. His telegraph work was really a side line.

"On these accounts he found a job as night operator at

Stratford Junction, Canada West, as Ontario was then called. He was only sixteen but his salary of twenty-five dollars a month seemed very small after making ten or twelve dollars a day as 'candy butcher.' But on account of the chances it gave him for experimenting, he resigned himself to the smallness of his pay. The treatment he had received at the hands of that train conductor had convinced him that he could not follow his bent while working all day on the railroad.

"Mr. Edison likes to tell of the prevailing ignorance of the science of telegraphy. He once told a friend:

"'The telegraph men themselves seemed unable to explain how the thing worked, though I was always trying to find out. The best explanation I got was from an old Scotch line repairer employed by the Montreal Telegraph Company, then operating the railway wires. Here is the way he described it: "If you had a dachshund long enough to reach from Edinburgh to London, and pulled his tail in Edinburgh he would bark in London!"

"'I could understand that, but I never could get it through me what went through the dog or over the wire.'

"It was at Stratford Junction that the Edison boy began his career of invention. From the first his chief aim was the saving of labor. In order to be sure that the operators all along the line were not asleep at their posts, they were required to send to the train dispatcher's office a certain dot-and-dash signal every hour in the night. Young Edison was like young Napoleon in grudging himself the necessary hours of sleep. While the ingenious lad was fond of machinery - to make a machine of himself was utterly distasteful to him. It was against his principles and instincts to do anything a mere machine could do instead. So he made a little wheel with a few notches in the rim, with which he connected the clock and the transmitter, so that at the required instant every hour in the night the wheel revolved and sent the proper signal to headquarters. Meanwhile that wily young operator slept the sleep of the genius, if not of the just. Of one experience at this little place Edison relates:

"'This night job just suited me, as I could have the whole day to myself. I had the faculty of sleeping in a chair any time for a few minutes at a time. I taught the night yardman my call, so I could get half an hour's sleep now and then between trains, and in case the station was called the watchman was to wake me. One night I got an order to hold a freight train, and I replied that I would do so. I ran out to find the signal man, but before I could locate him and get the signal set - *the train ran past!* I rushed back to the telegraph office and reported that I could not hold it.

"'But on receiving my first message that I would hold the freight, the dispatcher let another train leave the next station going the opposite way. There was a station near the Junction where the day operator slept. I started to run in that direction, but it was pitch dark. I fell down a culvert and was knocked senseless.'

"The two engineers, with a feeling that all was not as it should be, kept a sharp lookout and saw each other just in time to avert a fatal accident. But young Edison was cited to trial, for gross neglect of duty, by the general manager. During an informal hearing two Englishmen called on the manager. While he was talking with them the young night operator disappeared. Boarding a freight train bound for Port Sarnia, he made his escape from the five-years' term in prison threatened by the irate manager. Edison afterward confessed that his heart did not leave his throat until he had crossed the ferry to Port Huron and 'one wide river' lay between him and the Canadian authorities.

"Following his escape from Canada young Edison knocked about the home country, North and South. As it was during the Civil War he had some peculiar adventures. After making a long circuit, broken in many places by 'short circuits,' the journeyman telegrapher landed in Port Huron, and wrote his friend Adams, then in Boston to find him a job.

"His friend relates that he asked the Boston manager of the Western Union Telegraph office if he wanted a first-class operator from the West.

"'What kind of copy does he make?'" was the manager's first query. "Adams continues:

"'I passed Edison's letter through the window for his inspection. He was surprised, for it was almost as plain as print, and asked:

"'Can he take it off the wire like that?'

"'I said he certainly could, and that there was nobody who could stick him. He told me to send for my man and I did. When Edison came he landed the job without delay.'"

"The inventor himself has told the story of his reporting for duty in Boston:

"'The manager asked me when I was ready to go to work.

"'*Now!*' said I, and was instructed to return at 5:30 P.M., which I did, to the minute. I came into the operators' room and was ushered into the night manager's presence.

"'The weather was cold and I was poorly dressed; so my appearance, as I was told afterward, occasioned considerable merriment, and the night operators conspired to "put up a job on the jay from the wild and woolly West." I was given a pen and told to take the New York No. 1 wire. After an hour's wait I was asked to take my place at a certain table and receive a special report for the Boston *Herald*, the conspirators having arranged to have one of the fastest operators in New York send the despatch and "salt" the new man.

"'Without suspecting what was up I sat down, and the New

York man started in very slowly. Soon he increased his speed and I easily adapted my pace to his. This put the man on his mettle and he "laid in his best licks," but soon reached his limit.

"'At this point I happened to look up and saw the operators all looking over my shoulder with faces that seemed to expect something funny. Then I knew they were playing a trick on me, but I didn't let on.

"'Before long the New York man began slurring his words, running them together and sticking the signals; but I had been used to all that sort of thing in taking reports, so I wasn't put out in the least. At last, when I thought the joke had gone far enough, and as the special was nearly finished, I calmly opened the key and remarked over the wire to my New York rival:

"'Say, young man, change off and send with the other foot!'

"'This broke the fellow up so that he turned the job over to another operator to finish, to the real discomfiture of the fellows around me.'

"Friend Adams goes on to tell of other happennings at the Hub:

"'One day Edison was more than delighted to pick up a complete set of Faraday's works, bringing them home at 4 A.M. and reading steadily until breakfast time, when he said, with great enthusiasm:

"'Adams, I have got so much to do and life is so short, *I am going to hustle!*'"

"'Then he started off to breakfast on a dead run.'

"He soon opened a workshop in Boston and began making experiments. It was here that he made a working model of his vote recorder, the first invention he ever patented.

"Edison has told us of this trip to Washington and how he showed that his invention could register the House vote, pro and con, almost instantaneously. The chairman of the committee saw how quickly and perfectly it worked and said to him:

"'Young man, if there is any invention on earth that we *don't* want down here, it is this. Filibustering on votes is one of the greatest weapons in the hands of a minority to prevent bad legislation, and this instrument would stop that.'

"The youth felt the force of this so much that he decided from that time forth not to try to invent anything unless it would meet a genuine demand, - not from a few, but many people.

"It was while in Boston that Edison grew weary of the monotonous life of a telegraph operator and began to work up an independent business along inventive lines, so that he really began his career as an inventor at the Hub.

"After the vote recorder, he invented a stock ticker, and started a ticker service in Boston which had thirty or forty subscribers, and operated from a room over the Gold Exchange.

\*   \*   \*   \*   \*

"The third talk on Mr. Edison and his inventions will be given from this broadcasting station WUK next Monday at the same hour."

# CHAPTER VIII

## OPPORTUNITY KNOCKS

As the young people rose to depart, Professor Gray beckoned Bill and Gus to remain. He turned to a large table desk, took from it a roll of papers, untied and laid before the boys a number of neatly executed plans and sections - all drawn to scale. In an upper corner was pen-printed the words:

Water Power Electric Plant to be erected for and on the estate of Mr. James Hooper, Fairview. Engineer and Contractor, J. R. Gray.

"Boys, you see here," began the Professor, "the layout of a job to be done on the Hooper property. You know I do this sort of thing in a small way between school terms and I am told to go ahead with this at once. The amount I am to receive, on my own estimate, is ample, but naturally not very great; it covers all material, labor and a fair profit.

"But now," he went on, "comes the hitch. I am compelled, by another matter which is far more important, - having been appointed one of the consulting engineers on the Great Laurel Valley Power Plant, - to desert this job almost entirely, and yet, I am bound, on the strength of my word, to see that it is completed. If I hand it over to another engineer, or a construction firm, it will cost me more than I get out of it. And naturally, while I don't expect to gain a thing, I would prefer also not to lose anything. Now, what would you fellows advise in this matter?"

Bill looked at Gus and Gus looked at Bill; there was a world of meaning, of hope and hesitation, in both glances. The Professor saw this, and he spoke again:

"Out with it, boys! I asked you to stay, in order to hear what you might say about it. There seems to be only one logical solution. I cannot afford to spend a lot of my own money and yet I will gladly give all of my own profits, for I must complete Mr. Hooper's job and look after my bigger task at once."

"I don't suppose," said Gus, with the natural diffidence he often experienced in expressing his mind, "that we could help you."

"Why, of course we can, and we will, too," said Bill, the idea breakng on him suddenly. "We can carry on the work perfectly under your occasional direction. Is that what you wanted us to say, Professor?"

"I did. I hoped you would see it that way and I wanted you to acknowledge the incentive to yourselves. I am sure you can carry on the work, as you say. We have had enough of practical experimentation together, and then, what made me think of you, was that fish dam you put in for old Mr. McIlvain last summer."

The boys glanced at each other again, but this time with mutual feelings of pride. Bill had interested a well-to-do farmer in making a pool below a fine spring and with his consent and some materials he had furnished. The boys had stonewalled a regular gulch, afterwards stocking the crystal clear pool they had made with landlocked salmon obtained from the state hatchery. The fish were now averaging a foot in length and many a fine meal the boys and the farmer had out of that pond.

"Now, fellows, I'll divide between you the entire profits,"

Professor Gray began, but Bill and Gus both stopped him.

"No, sir! You pay us no more than we could have got in the mill, and the rest is yours. Look at the fun we'll have, that's worth a lot." Bill always tried to be logical and he never failed to have a reason for his conclusions. "And then," he added, "this will be for you and we couldn't do enough -"

"I'll see that you are paid and thank you, also," laughed the Professor. "And tomorrow morning, if it suits you, we shall start with the work, which means making a survey of the ground and listing materials. There will be a segment dam, with flood gates; about an eighth of a mile of piping; a Pelton wheel, boxed in; a generator speeded down; a two-horse-power storage battery; wiring and connections made with present lighting system in house; lodge; stables and garage; - and the thing is done if it works smoothly. The closest attention to every detail, taking the utmost pains, will be necessary and I know you will -"

"Just like Edison!" Bill fairly shouted, making Professor Gray and Gus laugh heartily. The Professor said:

"Eight! And we shall hope to follow his illustrious example. Tomorrow it is, then."

When the two chums, elated over their sudden advancement to be professional engineers, came out on the street, they were not a little surprised to see all the girls and boys of the class waiting, and evidently for them, as they could but judge on hearing the words:

"Here they come! We'll get him started. Bill knows."

# CHAPTER IX

## GUS HOLDS FORTH AGAIN

"Say, old scout," cautioned Gus, in a low voice, "better not tell about our job. Let it dawn on them later."

"Righto, Gus. It's nobody's business but ours. But what do the bunch want?"

Bill soon found out, however, when Cora and Ted came to meet him.

"We've had an argument, Terry and I, about Edison," said the girl, "and I know you can settle it. I said that -"

"Hold on! Don't tell me who said anything; then it'll be fair," Bill demanded.

"'O wise, wise judge!'" gibed Ted. "Ought to have a suit of ermine. Proper stunt, too. Let me put it, Cora; I'll be the court crier. Come on and let's squat on the bank like the rest. Judge, you ought to be the most elevated. Now, then, here's the dope: Did Edison really ever do anything much to help with the war?"

"He did more than any other man," Bill declared promptly. "Positively! Everybody ought to know that. He invented a device so that they could smell a German submarine half a mile away, and they could tell when a torpedo was fired.

Another invention turned a ship about with her prow facing the torpedo, so that it would be most likely to go plowing and not hit her, as it would with broadside on. I guess that saved many a ship and it helped to destroy lots of submarines with depth bombs. It got the Germans leery when their old submersibles failed to get in any licks and went out never to come back; it was as big a reason as any why they were so ready to quit. Well, who was right?"

"I was!" announced Cora, gleefully. "Terry just can't see any good in Edison at all. He says he hires people who really make his inventions and he gets the credit for them. He says -"

"I don't suppose it makes much difference what he says; he simply doesn't know what he's talk -"

"You think you know, but do you? You've read a lot of gush that -" Terry began, but Gus interrupted him, almost a new thing for the quiet chap.

"Listen, Terry: get right on this. Don't let a lot of foolish people influence you; people who can't ever see any real good in success and who blame everything on luck and crookedness. And Bill does know."

"Anybody who tries to make Edison out a small potato," declared Bill, addressing the others, rather than the supercilious youth who had maligned his hero, "is simply ignorant of the facts. My father knew a man well who worked for Edison in his laboratory for years. He said that the stories about Edison making use of the inventions of others is all nonsense; it is Edison who has the ideas and who starts his assistants to experimenting, some at one thing, some at another, so as to find out whether the ideas are good.

"He said that the yarns they tell about Edison's working straight ahead for hours and hours without food and sleep, then throwing himself on a couch for a short nap and getting up to go at it again are all exactly true, over and over again. He said that one of the boys in the shop tried to play a trick on the old man, as they call him, while he was napping on the couch. They rigged up a talking-machine on a stand and dressed it in some of Edison's old clothes, put a lullaby record on it, lugged it in, set it up in front of the couch and set it going, to express the idea that he was singing himself to sleep. But while they were at this Mr. Edison, getting on to the joke, for he generally naps with one eye open, got up and put a lot of stuffing under the couch spread, stuck his old hat on it so as to make it look as though his face was covered; then peered through the crack of a door. When the music commenced he opened the door and said:

"'Boys, it won't work; music can't affect dead matter.' Then they pulled off the couch cover and all had a good laugh.

"Now. you can see," Bill went on, with ever increasing enthusiasm, "just how that shows where Mr. Edison stands. Nobody can get ahead of him, and there isn't anyone with brains who knows him who doesn't admit he has more brains and is wider awake than anybody else. There's nothing that he does that doesn't show it. You have all seen his questionnaires for the men who are employed in his laboratories and you can bet they're no joke. And his inventions - they're not just the trifling things like egg-beaters, rat-traps, coat-hangers, bread-mixers, fly-swatters and lipsticks."

"But some of these things are mighty cute and they coin the dough," said Ted.

"Oh, they're ingenious and money-makers some of them, I'll admit, but we could get along very well without them and most of us do. But think of the real things Edison has done. The first phonograph; improving the telegraph so that six messages can be sent over the same wire at the same time; improving the telephone so that everybody can use it; collecting fine iron ore from sand and dirt by magnets; increasing the power and the lightness of the storage battery. And there are the trolleys and electric railways that have been made possible. And the incandescent electric lamp - how about that? Edison has turned his wonderful genius only to those things that benefit millions of -"

"And he deserved to make millions out of it," said Ted.

"I guess he has, too," offered one of the girls.

"You bet, and that's what he works for: not just to benefit people," asserted Terry.

"I suppose your dad and most other guys got their dough all by accident while they were trying to help other folks; eh?" Bill fired at Terry.

But the rich boy walked away, his usual method to keep from getting the worst of an argument.

"Oh, I wish Grace Hooper were here," Cora said. "She's no snob like Terry and wouldn't she enjoy this?"

"And her dad, too. Isn't he a nice old fellow, even though he's awfully rich?" laughed Dot.

"He'd have his say about this argument, grammar or no grammar. He thinks a lot of this chap he calls Eddy's son," Mary Dean declared.

"Great snakes! Does he really think the wizard is the child of some guy named Eddy?" Ted queried.

"Sounds so," Cora said. "But you can't laugh at him, he's so kind and good and it would hurt Grace. He would be interested in radio, too."

"Wonder he hasn't got a peach of a receiver set up in his house," Lucy Shore ventured.

"Is he keen for all new-fangled things?" asked Ted.

"You bet he is, though somebody would have to tell him and show him first. Well, people, I'm going home; who's along?"

With one accord the others got to their feet and started up or down the street. Gus and Bill went together, as always; they had much to talk about.

# CHAPTER X

## BRASS TACKS

On the day following the radio lecture, true to his promise, Professor Gray led Bill and Gus to the broad acres of the Hooper estate and there, with the plans before them, they went over the ground chosen for the water-power site, comprehending every detail of the engineering task. Professor Gray was more pleased than surprised by the ready manner in which both lads took hold of the problem and even suggested certain really desirable changes.

Bill indicated a better position fifty yards upstream for the dam and he sketched his idea of making a water-tight flood gate which was so ingenious that the Professor became enthusiastic and adopted it at once.

After nearly a whole day spent thus along the rocky defiles of the little stream, eating their lunch beside a cold spring at the head of a miniature gulch, the trio of engineers were about to leave the spot when a gruff voice hailed them from the hilltop. Looking up they saw another group of three: an oldish man, a slim young fellow who was almost a grown man and a girl in her middle teens. The young people seemed to be quarreling, to judge from the black looks they gave each other, but the man paid them no attention. He beckoned Professor Gray to approach and came slowly down the hill to meet him, walking rather stiffly with a cane.

"Well, Professor, you're beginnin' to git at it, eh? Struck any snags yit? Some job! I reckon you're not a goin' to make a heap outside the price you give me. When you goin' to git at it reg'lar?"

"Right away, Mr. Hooper. To-morrow. We have been making our plans to-day and these young assistants of mine, who will principally conduct the work, are ready to start in at once. They -"

"Them boys? No, sir! I want this here work done an' done right; no bunglin'. What's kids know about puttin' in water wheels an' 'letric lights? You said you was -"

"These boys are no longer just kids, Mr. Hooper, and they know more than you think; all that is needed to make this job complete. Moreover, I am going to consult with them frequently by letter and I shall be entirely responsible. It is up to me, you know."

Mr. Hooper evidently saw the sense in this last remark; he stood blinking his eyes at Bill and Gus and pondering. The slim youth plucked at his sleeve and said something in a low voice.

Gus suddenly remembered the fellow. The youth had come into the town a week or two before. He had, without cause, deliberately kicked old Mrs. Sowerby's maltese cat, asleep on the pavement, out of his way, and Gus, a witness from across the street, had departed from his usually reticent mood to call the human beast down for it. But though Gus hoped the fellow would show resentment he did not, but walked on quickly instead.

Mr. Hooper listened; then voiced a further and evidently suggested opposition:

"Them lads is from the town here; ain't they? Nothin' but a lot o' hoodlums down yan. You can't expec' -"

"You couldn't be more mistaken, Mr. Hooper. I'll admit there are a lot of young scamps in Fairview, but these boys, William Brown and Augustus Grier, belong to a more self-respecting bunch. I'll answer for them in every way."

"Of course, Dad, Professor Gray knows about them. Billy and Gus are in our class at school." This from the girl who had joyfully greeted the Professor and the boys, yodeling a school yell from the hillside. Then she shot an aside at the slim youth: "You're a regular, downright simpleton, Thad, and forever looking for trouble. Don't listen to him, Dad."

This appeared to settle the matter. Mr. Hooper squared his shoulders and grinned broadly, adding: "Well, I ain't just satisfied 'bout them knowin' how, but go to it your own way, Professor. I'm a goin' to watch it, you know; not to interfere with your plans an' ways, but it's got to be done right. If it goes along free an' fine, I ain't goin' to kick."

The Professor explained that they had further work to do on the plans and must be going back. He took leave of Mr. Hooper and the daughter, and retreated with the boys as hurriedly as Bill could manage his handy crutch. They all proceeded silently in crossing the broad field, but when in the road Bill had to voice his thoughts:

"I expect that old fellow'll make it too hot for us."

"Not for a minute; you need not consider that at all. Of course it would be more satisfactory if Mr. Hooper could be assured at once of your real ability, but it will have to grow on him. Just let him see what you can do; that's all."

"I rather expect we can frame up something that will satisfy him and Bill can spring it," said Gus.

"In just what way, can you imagine?" queried the Professor.

"Some geometrical stunt, maybe; triangulation, or -"

"Why, sure! That's just it!" exploded Bill. "I know how we can get him: Parallax! Shucks, it'll be easy! Just leave it to me."

"Looks as though some kind of Napoleonic strategy were going to be pulled off," asserted Professor Gray, laughing. "But, boys, keep in mind that Mr. Hooper, while a rough-and-ready old chap, with a big fortune made in cattle dealing, is really an uncut diamond; a fine old fellow at heart, as you will see."

# CHAPTER XI

## ENGINEERING

Two busy days followed during which Bill and Gus went to the city with Professor Gray to purchase materials in full for the power plant. They also had cement, reinforcing iron, lumber for forms and a small tool house hauled out to the power site and they drove the first stakes to show the position of wheel and pipe line. Mr. Hooper did not put in an appearance.

On the third morning the Professor bade the boys good-by, exacting the promise that they would write frequently of their progress. They had privately formed an engineering company with Professor Gray as president, Gus as vice-president, which was largely honorary, and Bill as general manager and secretary. Advance payments necessary for extra labor and their own liberal wages were deposited at the Fairview Bank by Professor Gray and the boys were given a drawing account thereon, with a simple expense book to keep.

That afternoon, dressed in new overalls and blouses, with a big, good-natured colored man to help with the laboring work, the boys were early on the job, at first making a cement mixing box; then Bill drove the center stake thirty feet below where the dam was to be placed and from which, using a long cord, the curve of the structure twenty-nine feet wide, was laid out upstream.

At the spot chosen the rock-bound hillsides rose almost perpendicularly from the narrow level ground that was little above the bed of the stream; it was the narrowest spot between the banks. George, the colored fellow, was set to work digging into one bank for an end foundation; the other bank held a giant boulder.

The boys were giving such close attention to their labors that they did not see observers on the hilltop. Presently the gruff voice that they had heard before hailed them from close by and they looked up to see Mr. Hooper and the slim youth approaching. The boys had heard that this Thaddeus was the old man's nephew and that he called the Hooper mansion his home.

"What you drivin' that there stake down there for? Up here's where the Perfesser said the dam was to set," Mr. Hooper demanded.

"Yes, right here," Bill replied. "But it is to be curved upstream and that stake is our center."

"What's the idea of curvin' it?"

"So that it will be stronger and withstand the pressure. You can't break an arch, you know, and to push this out the hills would have to spread apart."

"I kind o' see." The old man was thoughtful and looked on silently while the dam breast stakes were being driven every three feet at the end of a stretched cord, the other end pivoting on the center stake below, this giving the required curve.

"How deep you goin' into that hill? Seems like the water can't git round it now." Mr. Hooper, at a word from Thad, seemed inclined to criticize.

"We must get a firm end, preferably against rock," Bill explained.

"Shucks! Reckon the clay ain't goin' to give none. How much fall you goin' to git on that Pullet wheel?"

"Pelton wheel. About eighty feet, Professor Gray figured it roughly. We'll take it later exactly."

"Kin you improve on the Perfesser?"

"No, but he made only a rough calculation. We'll take it both by levels and by triangulation, using an old sextant of the Professor's. It isn't a diff -"

"What's try-angleation?" Mr. Hooper was becoming interested.

"The method of reading angles of different degrees and in that way getting heights and distances. That's the way they measure mountains that can't be climbed and tell the distance of stars."

"Shucks, young feller! I don't reckon anybody kin tell the distance o' the stars; they only put up a bluff on that. They ain't no ackshall way o' gittin' distance onless you lay a tape measure, er somethin' like it on the ground. These here surveyors all does it; I had 'em go round my place."

Bill smiled and shook his head. "I guess you just haven't given it any consideration. There are lots of easier and better ways. Triangulation. Now, for instance, suppose an army comes to a wide river and wants to get across. They can't send anybody over to stretch a line; there may be enemy sharp-shooters that would get them and it is too wide, anyway. But they must know how many pontoon boats and how much flooring plank they must have to bridge it and so they sight a tree or a rock on the other shore and take the distance across by triangulation. Or suppose -"

"Never heard of it. Why wouldn't surveyors git from here to yan that a-way, 'stead o' usin' chains? Could you - ?"

"Chaining it is a little more accurate, where they have a lot of curves and angles and the view is cut off by woods and hills. Yes, we can work triangulation; we could tell the distance from the hilltop to your house if we could see it and we had the time."

"Bunk! Don't let 'em bluff you that a-way, Uncle. Make 'em prove it." Thad showed his open hostility thus.

Gus dropped his shovel and came from the creekside where he had begun to dig alongside of the stakes for the foundation. He was visibly and, for him, strangely excited as he walked up to Thad.

"See here, fellow, Bill can do it and if there is anything in it we will do it, too! You are pretty blamed ignorant!"

Mr. Hooper threw back his head and let out a roar of mirth. "Well, I reckon that hits me, too. An' I reckon it might be true in a lot o' things. But Thad an' me, we kind o' doubt this."

"We sure do. I'd bet five dollars you couldn't tell it within half a mile an' it ain't much more than that."

"I'll take your bet and dare you to hold to it," said Gus.

"Bet 'em, Thad; bet 'em! I'll stake you."

"Oh, we don't want your money; betting doesn't get anywhere and it isn't just square, anyway." Bill was smilingly endeavoring to restore good feeling. "Now, Mr. Hooper, we're not fixed to make a triangulation measurement to-day, but -"

"Not fixed? Of course not. Begins with excuses," sneered Thad.

"But to-morrow we'll bring out Professor Gray's transit and show you the way it's done."

"Oh, yes, Uncle; they'll show us - to-morrow, or next day, or next week. Bunk!" Thad was plainly trying to be offensive.

"You'll grin on the other side of your hatchet face, fellow, when we do show you," said Gus.

"Now, Gus, cut out the scrapping. You can't blame him, nor Mr. Hooper, for doubting it if they've never looked into the matter. We can bring the transit out this afternoon for taking the levels. Be here after dinner, Mr. Hooper, if you can."

"I'll be here, lads," said the ex-cattle-dealer. "An' I reckon my nephew'll come along, too."

# CHAPTER XII

## DISTANCE LENDS ENCHANTMENT

Mr. Hooper, his nephew, his daughter and another girl, fat and dumpy, were at the power site before two o'clock, and without more ado Bill asked Gus to bring the transit to the comparatively level field on top of the hill.

"Now, Mr. Hooper, please don't think we're doing this in a spirit of idle controversy; we only want to show you something interesting."

"That's all right, lad; an' I ain't above learnin', old as I am. But Thad here, he's different." Mr. Hooper gave Bill and Gus a long wink. "Thad, he don't reckon he can be learned a thing, an' he's so blame sure - say, Thad, how 'bout that bet?"

"We don't want to bet anything; that only -" began Bill, but Gus was less pacific.

"Put up, or shut up," he said, drawing a borrowed five dollar note out of his pocket and glaring at Thad. The slim youth did not respond.

"He's afraid to bet," jeered the daughter. "Hasn't got the nerve, or the money."

"I ain't afraid to bet." Thad brought forth a like amount in bills. "Uncle'll hold the stakes. You got to tell how far it is from here to the house without ever stepping the distance."

"We'll make a more simple demonstration than that," Bill declared. "It'll be the same thing and take less time and effort. Mr. Hooper, take some object out there in the field; something that we can see; anything."

"Here, Gracie, you take a stake there an' go out yan an' stick it up. Keep a-goin' till I holler."

Both girls carried out these directions, the fat one falling down a couple of times, tripped by the long grass and getting up shaking with laughter. The boys were to learn that she was a chum of Grace Hooper, that her name was Sophronia Doyle, though commonly nicknamed "Skeets."

The stake was placed. Bill drove another at his feet, set the transit over it, peeped through it both ways and at his direction, after stretching the steel tape, Gus drove a third stake exactly sixty feet from the transit at an angle of ninety degrees from a line to the field stake.

"Now, folks," explained Bill, "the stake out yonder is A, this one is B and the one at the other end of the sixty-foot base line is C. Please remember that."

The transit was then placed exactly over the stake C and, peeping again, Bill found the angle from the base line to the stake B and the line to stake A to be 78 degrees. Thereupon Gus produced a long board, held up one end and rested the other on a stake, while Bill went to work with a six-foot rule, a straight edge and a draughtsman's degree scale. Bill elucidated:

"Now, then, to get out of figuring, which is always hard to understand, we'll just lay the triangulation out by scale, which is easily understood. One-eighth of an inch equals one foot. This point is stake B and the base line to C is this line at right angles, or square across the board. C stake is 7-1/2 inches from B which is equal to sixty feet on the scale, that is sixty one-eighth inches. Now, this line, parallel to the edge of the board, is the exact direction of your stake A. Do you all follow that?

"The direction to your stake was 78 degrees from the base line at C. This degree scale will give us that." Bill carefully centered the latter instrument, sharpened his pencil and marked the angle; then placing the straight edge on the point C and the degree mark he extended the line until it crossed the other outward line. At this crossing he marked a letter A and turned to his auditors.

"This is your stake out yonder. The rule shows it to be a little over 34-5/8 inches from the base line at B. That is, by the scale, a few inches over 277 feet and that is the distance from here to where Grace stuck it into the ground. Our hundred-foot steel tape line is at your service, Mr. Hooper."

Mr. Hooper merely glanced at Bill. He took up the tape line and spoke to his nephew. "Git a holt o' this thing, Thad, an' let's see if -"

Grace interrupted him. "No, Dad; never let Thad do it! He'd make some mistake accidentally on purpose. I'll help you."

There was utter silence from all while Grace carried out the end of the tape and placed her sticks, Mr. Hooper following after. Skeets borrowed a pencil and a bit of paper from Gus and went along with Grace to keep tally, but she dropped the pencil in the grass, stepped on and broke it, was suffused with embarrassment and before she could really become useful, the father and daughter had made the count mentally and they came back to the base line, still without saying a word, a glad smile on the girl's face and something between wonder and surprise on the old man's features.

Still without a word Mr. Hooper came straight to Bill, thrust out his big hand to grasp that of the smiling boy and in the other hand was held the bills of the wager, which he extended toward Gus.

"Yours, lad," he said. "We made the distance two hundred and seventy-eight foot. I reckon you git the money."

Thad stood for a moment, nonplussed, a scowl on his face. Suddenly he recovered.

"Hold on! That's more than they said it was. The money's mine."

"Shucks, you dumb fool! Maybe a couple o' inches. I reckon we made the mistake, fer we wasn't careful. It gits me they was that near it. The cash is his'n."

Gus took the bills, thrust his own into his pocket again and handed the two dollar note and the three ones to Skeets.

"Please give them to him for me," indicating Thad, "I don't want his money."

"Not I," said the fat girl; "it isn't my funeral. Let him do the weeping and you take and give them to the poor."

Gus offered them to Grace, who also refused, shaking her head. Bill took the bills, and, limping over to Thad, handed him his wager. "You mustn't feel sore at us," counseled the youthful engineer. "This was only along the lines of experiment and - and fun."

But though Bill meant this in the kindliest spirit of comradeship, the boy sensed a feeling of extreme animosity that he was at a loss to account for. Bill backed off, further speech toward conciliation becoming as lame as his leg. The others witnessed this and Grace said, quite heatedly:

"Oh, you can't make a silk purse out of a pig's ear. Thad's an incurable grouch," at which Skeets laughed till she shook, and Mr. Hooper nodded his head.

"Lad," he said, "you're a wonder an' I ain't got no more to say ag'in' your doin' this work here. Go ahead with it your own way. But this I am abossin': to-morrow's half day, I reckon, so both o' you come over to the house nigh 'long about noon an' set at dinner with us. You're more'n welcome."

# CHAPTER XIII

## COUNTER INFLUENCES

Thereafter, having been fully convinced by the demonstration and fully assured of the precise accuracy in the work on the power plant, Mr. Hooper treated the boys with the utmost consideration and confidence. The owner of the great estate came down to see them every day and chatted as familiarly as though he had been a lifelong crony of their own age. From time to time the boys were taken to dinner at the big house; they were given access to the library, and they found some time for social and sportive pastimes with the young folks whom Grace invited to her home.

Throughout all this Bill shone as an entertainer, a mental uplift that was really welcome, so spontaneous and keen were his talks and comments on people and things. Gus, though having little practice, held his own at tennis and golf; in swimming races and other impromptu sports he greatly excelled; and when a young fellow who bore the reputation of an all-round athlete came for the week-end from the city, Gus put on the gloves with him and punched the newcomer all over an imaginary ring on the lawn to the delight of Mr. Hooper, Grace and Skeets, as well as the admiring Bill.

Throughout all this, also, there was an element of ill feeling, an often open expression of antagonism toward the boys, which probably the other guests all tensed unpleasantly, but which the contented, jovial host and his impetuous and volatile daughter hardly recognized or thought of. Thaddeus, the thin-faced, pale, stoop-shouldered, indolent, cigarette-smoking nephew, though often treated with slight courtesy, continually pushed himself to the front, compelling consideration apparently for the sole purpose of exerting a counter-influence upon the popularity of Bill and Gus, especially the latter. The youth even went so far at times as to attempt an interference in the power-plant work, declaring that it did not proceed rapidly enough and that certain methods were at fault, to all of which Mr. Hooper turned a deaf ear.

There was nothing else but open warfare between Grace and Thad, Skeets also echoing the daughter's hostility, while the nephew easily pretended to ignore it, or to regard the sharp words aimed at him as jokes. He treated Skeets with as much contempt as her jovial manner permitted, but now and then it could be seen that his pale eyes glared at Grace's back in a way that seemed almost murderous.

One day Gus and George, the colored man, were working at the far end of the curved dam breast, the stone work having risen to four feet in height. Bill was stooping to inspect the cement on the near end and the view of the hill was cut off. Presently voices came to him, mostly a sort of good-natured protest in monosyllables; then Thad's tones, low enough to keep Gus from hearing.

"I tell you, Uncle, they're putting it over on you. It ain't any of my business, but I hate to see you having your leg pulled."

"'Taint!" was the brief answer.

"Well, if you don't want to think so; but I know it. Look at this dam: not over two feet thick and expected to hold tons of water. Wait till a flood hits it. Will it go out like a stack of cards, or won't it? And they're not using enough cement; one-fourth only with the sand."

"Grouting, broken stones," growled Mr. Hooper.

"Not sufficient, as you'll see. And does anybody want to say that a two-inch pipe is going to run a water wheel with force enough to turn a generator that will drive thirty or forty lights? Bosh!"

"They ought to know."

"You think they do, but have you any proof of it? What they don't know would fill a libra -"

"How 'bout that there triang - what you call it? They knew that."

"Oh, just a draughtsman's smart trick; used to catch people. I'm talking about things that are practical. You'll see. I'll bet you these blamed fools are going to strike a snag one of these days, or they'll leave things so that there'll be a fall-down. But what need they care after they get their money?"

Bill heard footsteps retreating and dying away; Mr. Hooper went over to Gus and, with evident hesitation, asked:

"Do you reckon you're makin' the stone work thick enough? It does look most terrible weak."

"Sure, Mr. Hooper. Bill'll explain that to you. Professor Gray and he worked out the exact resistance and the pressure."

And then Bill limped over; he had left his crutch on the hillside, and he said, half laughing:

"This wall, Mr. Hooper, can't give way, even if it had the ocean behind it, unless the stone and cement were mashed and crumbled by pressure. The only thing that could break it would be about two days' hammering with a sledge, or a big charge of blasting powder, and even that couldn't do a great deal of damage."

"All right, me lad; you ought to know an' I believe you."

Mr. Hooper's genial good humor returned to him immediately; it was evident that he was from time to time unpleasantly influenced by the soft and ready tongue of his nephew. The old gentleman turned toward home and disappeared; a short time afterward Thad came and stood near where Gus was working, but he said nothing, nor did Gus address him. Then the slim youth also departed and hardly half an hour elapsed before down the hill came Grace and Skeets, the latter stumbling several times, nearly pitching headlong and yet most mirthful over her own near misfortune; but little Miss Hooper seemed unusually serious-minded. A lively exchange of jests and jolly banter commenced between Skeets and Gus, who could use his tongue if forced to; but presently Grace left her laughing chum and came over to where Bill had resumed his inspection.

"They can't hear us, can they?" she queried, glancing back at the others.

"Why, I expect not," Bill replied, surprised and mystified.

"If I say something to you, real confidentially, you won't give me away, will you? Honest, for sure?"

"Honest, I won't; cross my heart; wish I may die; snake's tongue; butcher knife bloody!"

"That ought to do, and anybody with any sense would believe you, anyway. But, then, it will be a big temptation for you -"

"Resistance is my nickname; you may trust me."

"Well, then, in some way," said the girl, dropping her voice still lower, "you are going to find that this work here won't be - it won't go - not just as you expect it to; it - it won't be just plain sailing as it ought to be and would be if you were let alone. There are things," she put a forceful accent on the last word, "that will interfere - oh, sometimes dreadfully, maybe, and I felt that I must tell you, but -"

Bill, wondering, glanced up at her; she stood with her pretty face turned away, a troubled look in her bright eyes, the usually smiling lips compressed with determination. The boy's quick wits began to fathom the drift of her intention and the cause thereof; he must know more to determine her precise attitude.

"I must believe that you mean this in real kindness and friendliness toward Gus and me."

"Of course I do; else I would not have told you a thing," Grace said, blushing a little.

"I think it must be something real and that you know. This thing, then, as you call it, is more likely a person - some person who is working against us. You mean that; don't you?"

"Please don't ask me too much. I think you're very quick and intelligent and that you'll find out and be on your guard."

"I think I understand. Naturally you must feel a certain loyalty toward a relation, or at least if not just that, toward one who has your father's good will. Gus and I surely appreciate your warning; you'll want me to tell him, of course."

"I don't know. Gus is not so cool-headed as you are; I was afraid he might -"

"Trust Gus. He and I work together in everything. And I do thank you, Grace, more than I can express. Well keep our eyes open."

# CHAPTER XIV

## FURTHER OPPOSITION

The dam was built, the flood gate in place, the pipe valve set for further extension of the line down the little valley; and as the pipe had all come cut and threaded, Bill and George were working with wrenches and white lead to get the sections tightly jointed against the pressure that would result. Gus, the carpenter, was laying out the framing of heavy timbers reinforced with long bolts and set in cement on which the Pelton wheel was to be mounted.

Several days were thus spent; the water was pouring over the spillway of the dam and it was with satisfaction that the boys found, after an inspection one quitting hour, that the wall, five feet high, was not leaking a drop.

That night Gus came over to Bill's home and the two went over the plans until late; then Gus chatted awhile on the steps, Bill standing in the doorway. Suddenly, from over toward the northeast, in the direction of the upper tract of the Hooper estate, there was a flash in the sky and a dull reverberation like a very distant or muffled blast. Bill was talking and hardly noticed it, but Gus had been looking in that direction and, calling Bill's attention, wondered as to the cause of the odd occurrence.

In the morning, as the boys descended the hill, George, who was always on hand half an hour ahead of time, came up to

Wayne Whipple and S. F. Aaron

meet them and was plainly excited.

"Mist' Bill an' Gus, de dam's done busted a'ready an' de water's jes' a-pourin' through t' beat ol' Noah's flood! Whut you 'low was de because o' dis givin' way?"

"By cracky, Bill!" was Gus' comment as they stood looking at the break which seemed to involve a yard square of the base and cracks, as though from a shock. "You know and I know that the water didn't push this out. How about that flash and bang we heard last night?"

"I can't see how the water could have done it," said Bill, who evidently had more talent for construction than for determining destruction.

"There's something behind this that I don't like and I'm going to find out about it," said Gus, his usually quiet demeanor entirely gone. "You ought to be able," he continued, "to put two and four together. How about that warning Grace gave you? And how did she know anything out of which to give it? And why wouldn't she give any names?"

"Well, I have wondered; I thought I saw why," Bill said.

"Of course you see why, old scout. And if you'll leave it to me, you'll know why and all the how and the what of it, too." Gus was never boastful; now he was merely determined.

The boys opened the flood gate and after the water no longer flowed through the break, they began a closer examination that surprised them. Mr. Hooper, Thad, Grace and Skeets descended the hill.

Bill, after greetings, merely pointed to the break. Mr. Hooper started to say something about the structure's being too weak; Thad laughed, and Grace, looking daggers at him, turned away and pulled Skeets with her. Gus, gazing at Thad, addressed Mr. Hooper.

"Yes, too weak to stand the force of an explosion. It wasn't the water pressure. Mr. Hooper; you'll notice that the stones there are forced in against the water; not out with it. And the cracks - they're further evidence. We heard the explosion about eleven o'clock; saw the light of the flash, too."

"Shucks! You reckon that's so? Got any notion who it was that done it?"

"Yes, sir; got a big notion who it was; but we won't say till we get it on him for sure. And then's it's going to be a sorry day for him."

Gus was still gazing straight at Thad and that youth, first attempting to ignore this scrutiny and then trying to match it, at last grew restless and turned away. Mr. Hooper also had his eyes on Thad; the old gentleman looked much troubled. He raised his voice loud enough for Thad to hear as he walked off:

"We'll git a watchman an' put him on the job, - that's what we'll do! They ain't goin' to be any more o' this sort o' thing."

And Bill chimed in: "Good idea. There's George, Mr. Hooper; we're nearly through with him and we've been wondering what to put him at, for we'd be sorry to lose him."

So it was arranged then and there, much to the satisfaction of everyone, especially the old darkey, and Mr. Hooper, saying nothing more but looking as though there were a death in his family, started away toward home.

# CHAPTER XV

## MR. EDDY'S SON'S SONS

It took but a short time to repair the break; before many other days had passed the Pelton wheel, a direct action turbine, was going at a tremendous rate, driven by a nozzled stream from the pipe. It was necessary to belt it down from a small to a larger pulley to run the generator at a slower speed, which was 1200 a minute. Then came the boxing in, the wiring to the house, and the making of connections with the wiring to the house after the town company's service was dispensed with, and it was a proud moment when Gus turned on the first bulb and got a full and brilliant glare.

Mr. Hooper clasped the hands of both boys, compelled them to spend the evening, ordered special refreshments for the occasion, told Grace to invite a lot of the young folks and when, at dusk all the lights of the house went on with an illumination that fairly startled the guests, the host proposed a cheer for the boys which found an eager and unanimous response. Mr. Hooper attempted to make a speech, with his matronly and contented wife laughing and making sly digs at his effort, and his daughter encouraging him.

"Now, young fellers," he began, "these boys - uh, Mister Bill Brown an' Mister 'Gustus Grier, - I says to them, - in the first place, I says: 'Perfesser, these here kids don't know enough to build a chicken coop,' I says, an' Perfesser Gray he says to me, he says, he would back them fellers to build a battleship or tunnel through to Chiny, he says. So I says: 'You kids kin go ahead,' I says, an' these blame boys they went ahead an' shucks! you all see what they, Bill an' Gus, has done. You fellers has got to have a lot o' credit an' you are goin' to git it!

"Now, my wife she don't think I'm any good at makin' a speech an 'I ain't, but I'm a-makin' it jes' the same fer these boys, Bill an' Gus, b'jinks! They got to git credit fer what they done, jes' two kids doin' a reg'lar man's job. An' I reckon that not even that feller Eddy's son, that there chap they call the 'Wizard of Menlo Park,' I reckon he couldn't 'lectrocute nothin' no better'n these here boys, Bill an' Gus, has lighted this here domycile. An' - oh, you kin laugh, Ma Hooper, b'jinks, but I reckon you're as proud o' these here young Eddy's son's sons as I be. Now, Mister Bill an' Mister Gus, you kin bet all these folks'd like to have a few words. Now, as they say in prayer meetin', 'Mister Bill Brown'll lead us in a speech.' Hooray!"

Bill seized his crutch, got it carefully under his arm and arose. He was not just a rattle-box, a mere word slinger, for he always had something to say worth listening to; talking to a crowd was no great task for him and he had a genius for verbal expression.

"I hope my partner in mechanical effort and now in misery will let me speak for him, too, for he couldn't get up here and say a word if you'd promise him the moon for a watch charm. Our host, Mr. Hooper, would have given us enough credit if he had just stated that we were two persevering ginks, bent on making the best of a good chance and using, perhaps with some judgment, the directions of our superior, Professor Gray, along with some of our own ideas that fitted, in. But to compare us and our small job here, which was pretty well all mapped out for us, to the wonderful endeavors of Thomas Alva Edison is more than even our combined conceit can stand for. If we deserved such praise, even in the smallest way, you'd see us with our chests swelled out so far that we'd look like a couple of garden toads.

Wayne Whipple and S. F. Aaron

"Edison! Mr. Hooper, did you, even in your intended kindness in flattering Gus and myself, really stop to think what it could mean to compare us with that wonderful man? I know you could not mean to belittle him, but you certainly gave us an honor far beyond what any other man in the world, regarding electrical and mechanical things, could deserve. If we could hope to do a hundredth part of the great things Edison has done, it would, as Professor Gray says, indeed make life worth living.

"But we thank you, Mr. Hooper, for your kind words and for inviting all these good friends and our classmates, and we thank you and good Mrs. Hooper for this bully spread and everything!"

Bill started to sit down amidst a hearty hand-clapping, but Cora Siebold waved her hand for silence and demanded:

"Tell us more about Edison, Billy, as you did after the talk over the radio! You see, we missed the last of it and I'll bet we'd all like to hear more -"

"Yes!" "Yes!" "Sure!" "Me, too!" "Go on, Billy!" came from Dot Myers, Skeets, Grace Hooper, Ted Bissell and Gus. In her enthusiastic efforts at showing an abundant appreciation, the fat girl wriggled too far out on the edge of her chair, which tilted and slid out from under her, causing sufficient hilarious diversion for Bill to take a sneak out of the room. When Cora and Grace captured and brought him back, the keen edge of the idea had worn off enough for him to dodge the issue.

"I'll tell you what we're going to do," he said, and it will be better than anything we can think of just between us here. You all read, didn't you, that the lectures were to be repeated by request in two months after the last talk? We didn't hear it because Professor went away, and now three weeks of the time have gone by. But I'll tell you what Gus and I are going to do: we're going to build a radio receiver and get it done in time to get those talks on Edison all over again."

"Really?"

"Do you think you can do it?"

"If Billy says he can, why, the -"

"Oh, you Edison's son!" This from the irrepressible Ted.

"Go to it, Bill!"

"Can we all listen in?"

"Why, of course," said Bill, replying to the last question. "Everybody'll be invited and there will be a horn. But don't forget this: We've only got a little over four weeks to do it and it's some job! So, if you're disappointed -"

"We won't be."

"No; Bill'll get there."

"Hurrah for old Bill!"

"Say, people, enough of this. I'm no candidate for President of the United States, and remember that Gus is in this, too, as much as I am."

"Hurrah for Gus!" This was a general shout.

Gus turned and ran.

Wayne Whipple and S. F. Aaron

# CHAPTER XVI

## THE DOUBTERS

The party was on the point of breaking up, with much laughter over the embarrassment of poor Gus, when Skeets unexpectedly furnished further entertainment. She had paused to lean comfortably against a center table, but its easy rolling casters objected to her weight, rolled away hastily and deposited her without warning on the floor. Ted, who gallantly helped her to her feet, remarked, with a grunt due to extreme effort, that she really might as well stand up or enlist the entire four legs of a chair to support her.

Bill, about to take leave of the host and hostess, felt a slight jerk at his sleeve and looking round was surprised to find Thad at his elbow. The youth said in a low voice:

"Want to see you out yonder among the trees. Give the rest the slip. Got a pipe of an idea."

Bill nodded, wondering much. A moment later Mr. Hooper was repeating that he was proud of the work done by the boys and glad that he had trusted them. Then he added:

"But say, young feller, much as I believe in you and Gus, seein' your smartness, I got to doubt all that there bunk you give them young people 'bout that there what you call radier. I been borned a long time - goin' on to seventy year now, - an' I seen all sorts of contraptions like reapers an' binders, ridin' plows, typewritin'-machines, telephones, phonygraphs, flyin'-machines, submarines an' all such, but b'jinks, I ain't a-believin' that nobody kin hear jes' common talk through the air without no wires. An' hundreds o' miles! 'Tain't natch'all an' 'taint possible now, is it?"

"Why, yes, Mr. Hooper; it's both poss -"

"Come on, Billy! Good-night, Mr. Hooper and Mrs. Hooper. We all had a dandy time." And Bill was led away. But he was able, by hanging back a little, to whisper to Gus that he was on the track of something from Thad, - for Bill could only think that the young man would make a confession or commit himself in some way.

"See you in the morning," he added and turned back.

Thad was waiting and called to Bill from his seat on a bench beneath the shade of a big maple. The fellow plunged at once into his subject, evidently holding the notion that youth in general possesses a shady sense of honor.

"See here, Brown. I think I get you and I believe you've got wit enough to get Uncle Hooper. Did he say anything to you as you came out about being shy on this radio business?"

Bill nodded.

"Say, he don't believe it's any more possible than a horse car can turn into a buzzard! Fact! He told me you fellows might fool him on a lot of things and that you were awful smart for kids, but he'd be hanged for a quarter of beef if you could make him swallow this bunk about talking through the air. You know the way he talks."

"I think he can and will be convinced," said Bill, "and you can't blame him for his notion, for he has never chanced to inquire about radio and I expect he doesn't read that department in the paper. If he meets a plain statement about

　　　　Wayne Whipple and S. F. Aaron

radio broadcasting or receiving, it either makes no impression on him, or he regards it as a sort of joke. But, anyway, what of it?"

"Why, just this and you ought to catch on to it without being told: Unk's a stubborn old rat and he hasn't really a grain of sense, in spite of all the money he made. All you've got to do is to egg him on as if you thought it might be a little uncertain and then sort o' dare to make a big bet with him. I'll get busy and tell him that this radio business is the biggest kind of an expert job and that you fellows are blamed doubtful about it. Then, when you get your set working and let Unk listen in, he'll pay up and we'll divide the money. See? Easy as pie. Or we might work it another way: I'll make the bet with him and you fellows let on to fall down. Or we might -"

"Well, I've listened to your schemes," said Bill, "and I'm going to say this about them: I think you are the dirtiest, meanest skunk I ever ran across. You -"

"Say, now, what's the matter?"

"You're a guest under your uncle's roof; eating his grub, accepting his hospitality, pretending to be his friend -"

"Aw, cut that out, now! You needn't let on you're so awful fine."

"And then deliberately trying to hatch a scheme to rob him! Of all the rotten, contemptible -" Unable to voice his righteous indignation, Bill clenched his fist and struck Thad square in the eye.

Thad had risen and was standing in front of Bill, trembling with rage as impotent as though *he* were little and lame, leaning, like Bill, on the crutch a less valiant cripple would have used instead of his bare fist.

With a look of fiendish hatred, instead of returning blow for blow, Thad made a sudden grab and tore Bill's crutch out of the hand which had felt no impulse to use it in defense against his able-bodied antagonist.

"Now, you blow to Uncle and I'll break this crutch!"

Strange, isn't it, how we often are reminded of funny things even in the midst of danger? Bill, a cripple and unable to move about with the agility needed to fend off a cowardly attack by this miserable piker, showed the stuff he was made of when he burst out laughing, for he was reminded by this threat of that old yarn about a softy's threatening to break the umbrella of his rival found in the vestibule of his girl's house, then going out and praying for rain!

Thad, astonished at Bill's sudden mirth, held the crutch mid-air, and demanded with a malignant leer:

"Huh! Laugh, will you?"

"Go ahead and break it, but it won't be a circumstance to what I'll do to you. I can imagine your uncle -"

"So? Listen, you pusillanimous, knock-kneed shrimp? I'm going to mash your jaw so you'll never wag it again! And right now, too, you -"

Possibly there was as much determination back of this as any evil intent, but it also was doomed to failure. There was a quick step from the deeper shadows and a figure loomed suddenly in front of Thad who, with uplifted crutch, was still glaring at Bill. Only two words were spoken, a "*You*, huh?" from the larger chap; then a quick tackle, a short straining scuffle, and Thad was thrown so violently sidewise and hurtled against the bench from which Bill had just risen, that it and Thad went over on the ground together. The bench and the lad seemed to lie there equally helpless. Gus picked up the crutch and handed it to his chum.

"Let's go. He won't be able to get up till we've gone."

But as they passed out from among the shadows there followed them a threat which seemed to be bursting with the hatred of a demon:

"Oh, I'll get even with you two little devils. I'll blow you to -"

The two boys looked at each other and only laughed.

"Notice his right eye when you see him again," chuckled Bill.

# CHAPTER XVII

## THE UNEXPECTED

"Where did you come from, Gus?" Bill asked, still inclined to laugh.

"The road. Slipped away from the others for I was wondering whether you might not get into trouble. Couldn't imagine that chump would spring anything that wouldn't make you mad, and I knew you'd talk back. So I did the gumshoe."

"Well, I suppose he would have made it quite interesting for me and I am eternally grateful to you. If it weren't for you, Gus, I guess, I'd have a hard time in -"

"By cracky, if it weren't for you, old scout, where would I be? Nowhere, or anywhere, but never somewhere."

"That sounds to me something like what Professor Gray calls a paradox," laughed Bill.

"I don't suppose you're going to peach on Thad," Gus offered.

"No; but wouldn't I like to? It's a rotten shame to have that lowdown scamp under Mr. Hooper's roof. It's a wonder Grace doesn't give him away; she must know what a piker he is."

"Bill, it's really none of our business," Gus said. "Well, see you in the morning early."

The boys wished once more to go over carefully all the completed details of the water power plant; they had left the Pelton wheel flying around with that hissing blow of the water on the paddles and the splashing which made Bill think of a circular log saw in buckwheat-cake batter. The generator, when thrown in gear, had been running as smoothly as a spinning top; there were no leaks in the pipe or the dam. But now they found water trickling from a joint that showed the crushing marks of a sledge, the end of the nozzle smashed so that only enough of the stream struck the wheel to turn it, and there was evidence of sand in the generator bearings.

Then appeared George, with an expression of mingled sorrow, shame, wonder and injured pride on his big ebony features, his eyes rolling about like those of a dying calf. At first he was mute.

"Know anything about this business, George?" asked Bill.

"Don't know a thing but what Ah does know an' dat's a plenty. What's happened here?"

"The plant has been damaged; that's all."

"Damage? When? Las' night, close on t' mawnin'? Well, suh, Ah 'low that there ghos' done it."

"Ghost? What - where was any ghost?"

"Right yer at de tool house. Come walkin' roun' de corner fo' Ah could grab up man stick an' Ah jes' lef' de place."

"What? Ran away and from your duty? You were put here to guard the plant; not to let any old -"

"Didn't 'low t' guard it 'gainst no ghos'es. Dey don' count in de contrac'. Folks is one thing an' ghos'es -"

"Ghosts! Bosh! There's no such thing as a ghost! If you had

swung your club at the silly thing you'd have knocked over some dub of a man that we could pretty well describe right now, and saved us a heap of trouble and expense - and you'd have kept your job!" Bill was disgusted and angry.

"Lawsee! Ah ain't gwine lose mah job jes' fo' dodgin' a ghos', is I?"

"What did this fellow look like?" asked Gus.

"Ah nevah could tell 'bout it; didn't take no time for' t' look sharp. Ah wuz on'y jes' leavin'."

"Now, see here, George," said Bill, his native gentleness dominating, "if you'll promise to say nothing about this, keep on the job and grab the next ghost, we'll let you stay on. And we'll make an awful good guess when we tell you that you'll find the ghost is Mr. Hooper's nephew. If you do grab him, George, and lock him in the tool house, we'll see that you're very nicely rewarded, - a matter of cold cash. Are you on?"

"Ah shore is, an' Ah'll git him, fo' Ah reckon he's gwine come again. 'Tain't no fun tacklin' whut looks lak a ghos', but Ah reckon Ah'll make that smahty think he's real flesh an' blood fo' Ah gits through with him!"

The boys were two days making repairs, which time encroached upon their plan to get their promised radio receiver into action. Having no shop nor proper tools for finer work, they would be handicapped, for they had decided, because of the pleasure and satisfaction in so doing, to make many of the necessary parts that generally are purchased outright. Bill made the suggestion, on account of this delay, that they abandon their original plan, but Gus, ever hopeful, believed that something might turn up to carry out their first ideas.

The afternoon that they had everything in normal condition again, Mr. Hooper came down to see them; he knew nothing of the tampering with the work, but it became evident at once that his nephew had slyly and forcibly put it into his head that amateur radio construction was largely newspaper bunk, without any real foundation of fact. Thad may have had some new scheme, but at any rate the unlettered old m an wouldswallow pretty nearly everything Thad said, even though he often repudiated Thad's acts. Again Mr. Hooper, Bill and Gus got on the subject of radio and the old gentleman repeated his convictions:

"I ain't sayin' you boys can't do wonders, an' I'm fer you all the time, but I'm not goin' t' b'lieve you kin do what's pretty nigh out o' reason. Listen to me, now, fer a minute: If you fellers kin rig up a machine to fetch old man Eddy's son's talk right here about two hundred an' fifty mile, I'll hand out to each o' you a good hundred dollars; yes, b'jinks. I'll make it a couple a hun -"

"No, Mr. Hooper, we value your friendship altogether too much to take your money and that's too much like a wager, anyway." Bill was most earnest. "But you must take our word for it that it can be done."

"Fetch old man Eddy's son's voice - !"

"Just that exactly - similar things have been done a-plenty. People are talking into the radio broadcasters and their voices are heard distinctly thousands of miles. But, Mr. Hooper, you wouldn't know Mr. Edison's voice if you heard it, would you?"

"N - no, can't say as how I would - but listen here. I do know a feller what works with him - they say he's close to the ol' man. Bill Medders. Knowed Bill when he was a little cack, knee-high to a grasshopper. They say he wrote a book about Eddy's son. I'd know Bill Medder's voice if I heard it in a b'iler factory."

Bill Brown could hardly repress a smile. "I guess you must mean William H. Meadowcroft. His 'Boys' Life of Edison' sure is a dandy book. I liked it best of all. Sometimes no one can see Mr. Edison for weeks at a time, when he's buried in one of his 'world-beaters.' But I reckon we can let you hear Mr. Meadowcroft's voice. He wrote me a pippin of a letter once about the Chief."

"All righty. I'll take Medders's. I know Bill, an' you can't fool me on that voice."

"Mr. Hooper, I'll tell you what," said the all-practical Bill eagerly. "This demonstration will be almost as interesting to you as it is to us, and you can help us out. We can get what little power we need from any power plant. But we want a shop most of all - a loft or attic with room enough to work in. We're going to get all the tools we need -"

"No. I'll get 'em fer you an' you kin have all that there room over the garage." (The old gentleman pronounced this word as though it rhymed with carriage.) "An' anything else you're a mind to have you kin have. Some old junk up there, I reckon," he went on. "You kin throw it out, er make use of it. An' now, let's see what you kin do!"

The boys were eager to acknowledge this liberal offer, and they expressed themselves in no measured terms. They would do better than make one receiver; they would make two and one would be installed in Mr. Hooper's library, - but of this they said nothing at first. Get busy they did, with a zeal and energy that overmatched even that given the power plant. That afternoon they moved into the new shop and were delighted with its wide space and abundant light. The next day they went to the city for tools and materials. Two days later a lathe, a grinder and a boring machine, driven by a small electric motor wired from the Hooper generator were fully installed, together with a workbench, vises, a complete tool box and a drawing board, with its instruments. No young laborers in the vineyard of electrical fruitage could ask for more.

"Isn't it dandy, Gus?" Bill exclaimed, surveying the place and the result of their labors in preparation. "If we can't do things here, it's only our fault. Now, then -"

"It is fine," said Gus, "and we're in luck, but somehow, I think we must be on our guard. I can't get my mind off ghosts and the damage over yonder. I'm going to take a sneak around there to-night again, along around midnight and a little after. I did last night; didn't tell you, for you had your mind all on this. George was on duty, challenged me, but I've got a hunch that he knows something he doesn't want to worry us about and thinks he can cope with."

# CHAPTER XVIII

## A BIT TRAGIC

"Hold up your hands, nigger!"

The voice was low and sepulchral, but either the ghostly apparition that uttered the command had slipped up on its vernacular, or it was the spirit of a bandit. Some demand of the kind was, however, urgently necessary, for George did not, as formerly, show a desire to flee; his belligerent attitude suggested fight and he was a husky specimen with a handy club. Even though he might have suffered a qualm at again beholding the white apparition in the moonlight, his determination to dare the spectre was bolstered by the voice and the manner of the command.

"Ah knows who yo' is an' Ah's gwine hol' yo' up! Yo' ain't no ghos'. Dis club'll knock de sure 'nough breff out'n yo'; then we'll see."

To Gus, on the hillside above the power plant, it looked very much as though this threat were going to be carried out. He had been quietly observing, under the light of a half moon, the ghostly visitation and even the advent of this individual before the white raiment had been donned some distance behind the tool house and unknown to the watchful George. All this had not surprised Gus, but he had been puzzled by the appearance on the hillside of another figure that kept behind the scant bushes much as Gus was doing, except that it was screened against being seen from below and evidently did not know of Gus's presence. Now, however, all attention was given to the altercation before the tool house, around which the ghost had come, evidently to be disappointed at not seeing George take to his heels.

Suddenly there was a shot. The reverberation among the hills seemed ominous, but not more so than the staggering back and sinking down of poor George. Gus saw the white figure stand for a moment, as though peering down at the victim of this murderous act; then it turned and fled straight up the hill and directly toward the one up there crouching and - waiting? Were they in collusion? Gus had but a moment to guess. Still crouching, unseen, though brave, - for Gus was courageous even sometimes to the point of being foolhardy in the rougher sports, or where danger threatened others, - he avoided now the almost certain fate of George, for the villain was still armed and desperate, no doubt. And Gus hoped that the arrest of the scamp would surely follow his meeting with the other observer.

But this safe and sane attitude of the watching Gus suffered a sudden change when, as the ascending ruffian fairly stumbled upon the other figure crouching on the hillside, a scream, unmistakably that of a female in dire distress, came to the ears of the witness. He could dimly see the two struggling together, the dark figure with the white. The next instant, forgetting all danger to himself, Gus lessened the distance by leaps and scrambles along the declivity and flung himself upon the assailant.

There was a short, sharp tussle; a second shot, but this time the weapon discharged its leaden pellet harmlessly. Then the ghost, taking advantage of the hillside, flung Gus aside and before the boy had time to leap upon his foeman again, the white figure, his habiliments torn off, had backed away and threatened Gus with the pistol. There was no mistaking the voice that uttered the threat:

"Keep off, or you'll get punctured! You needn't think

anybody's going to get me. I'm going to vanish. If you try to follow me now, I'll kill you!"

This sounded desperate enough and Gus had reason to believe the fellow meant it. But in spite of that and driven by righteous anger, he would again have tackled the enemy had not the voice of Grace Hooper checked him:

"Oh, let him go; let him go!" she begged. "He'll shoot, and you - you
must not be killed! No; you shall not!"

And then, as the rascal turned and fled over the brow of the hill, Gus
turned to the girl, sitting on the ground.

"How did you come here - what - ?"

"I knew something was going to happen, and I thought I might prevent it some way. Then he fired, and I saw how desperate he was, - and he shot -"

"Yes - we must do all we can for poor George, if anything can be done. But are you hurt?"

"Not very much; he meant to hurt me. I dodged when he struck and only my shoulder may be - bruised."

"Then you should bathe it in hot water. Can I help you up? No, you must not go home alone - but I must see about poor George. I heard him groan."

"I'd better go down with you."

"It might be - too horrible - for a girl, you see. Better stay here."

Gus had extended his hand to give her a lift; she took it and came slowly to her feet; then suddenly crumpled up and lay

Wayne Whipple and S. F. Aaron

unconscious before him, her face white against the dark sod, her arms outflung. Gus stared at her a few long seconds, as foolishly helpless as any boy could be. He told Bill afterward that he never felt so flabbergasted in his life. What to do he knew not, but he must try something, and do it quickly. Perhaps Grace had only fainted; should he go to George first? He might be dying - or dead! Then the thought came to him: "Women and children first."

Gus dashed down the hill, dipped his cap, cup fashion, into the water of the dam and fled up with it again, brimming full and spilling over. He was able to dash a considerable quantity of reviving water into the girl's face. With a gasp and a struggle she turned over, opened her eyes, sat up, - her physical powers returning in advance of her mental grasp.

"Oh, am I, - no, not dead? Please help me - up and home."

"Yes, I'll take you home in just a jiffy. Do you feel a little better? Can you sit still here, please, till I see about George? Just a moment?"

Again the boy went down the hill, now toward the tool house; he was brave enough, but a sort of horror gripped him as he rounded the corner of the little shack. What, then, was his relief when he found the watchman on his feet, a bit uncertain about his balance and leaning against the door frame. It was evident from the way he held his club that he meant not to desert his post and that he believed his late assailant was returning. At sight of Gus, the colored man's relief showed in his drawn face.

"Mist' Gus! It's you, honey! My Lawd! Ah done been shot! By the ghos', Mist' Gus, whut ain't nothin' no mo'n dat low-down, no 'count nephew o' ol' Mist' Hooper's. Ah reckon Ah's gwine die, but Ah ain't yit - not ef he's comin' back!"

"Good boy, George! You're the stuff! But you're not going to die and he's not coming back. He lit out like a rabbit. Come now; we'll go to a doctor and then -"

"Reckon Ah can't do it. Got hit in de hip some'ers; makes mah leg total wuthless. You-all go on an' Ah'll git me some res' yere till mawnin'."

"And maybe bleed nearly to death! No, I'll be back for you in no time, - as soon as I get Miss Grace home. She's on the hill there. She came out to watch that cousin of hers. You hang on till I get back."

Grace tried to show her usual energy, but seemed nearly overcome by fatigue. She made no complaint, but presently Gus saw that she was crying, and that scared him. In his inexperience he could not know that it was only overwrought nerves. He felt he must make speed in carrying out his intentions to get help to George and put the authorities on the track of Thad. Gus could see but one thing to do properly and his natural diffidence was cast aside by his generous and kindly nature.

"Let me give you a lift, as I do Bill, sometimes," he said, and drew the girl's arm over his shoulder, supporting her with his other arm. In a second or two they were going on at a rather lively pace. In a few minutes they had reached the house. Grace entered and called loudly. Her father and mother appeared instantly in the hallway above. The girl, half way up the stairway, told of the incidents at the power plant and added:

"Thad boasted to me that he was going to give the boys a lot more trouble, and I watched and saw him leave the house. So I followed, hoping to stop him, and after he shot George he ran into me and was so angry that he struck me. I wish *I* had had a pistol! I would have -"

"Gracie, dear little girl! You mustn't wish to kill or wound anyone! Oh, are you *hurt*? Come, dear -"

"I'll be with you right off, me boy!" said Mr. Hooper to Gus, and presently they were in the library alone.

"Listen to me, lad. This nevvy o' mine is me dead sister's child, an' I swore t' her I'd do all I could fer him. His brother Bob, he's in the Navy, a decent lad; won't have nothin' to do with Thad. An' you can't blame him, fer Thad's a rapscallion. Smart, too, an' friendly enough to his old uncle. But now, though, I'm done with him. I'm fer lettin' him slide, not wantin' to put the law on him. I'll take care o' George. He shall have the best doctor in the country, an' I'll keep him an' his wife in comfort, but I don't want Thaddeus to be arrested. Now I reckon he's gone an' so let luck take him - good, bad, er indifferent. Won't you let him hit his own trail, foot-loose?"

"I'd like to see him arrested and jailed," said Gus, "but for you and because of what you'll do for George and your being so good to Bill and me, I'll keep mum on it."

"Good, me lad. An' now you git back to George an' tell him to keep Thad's name out of it. I'll 'phone fer 'Doc' Little and 'Doc' Yardley, an' have an ambulance sent fer the poor feller. Then you can tell his wife. It means very little sleep fer you this night, but you can lay abed late."

Gus went away upon these duties, but with a heavy heart; he felt that Mr. Hooper, because of the very gentleness of the man was defeating justice, and though he had been nearly forced to give his promise, he felt that he must keep it.

# CHAPTER XIX

## CONSTRUCTION AND DESTRUCTION

Bill and Gus worked long hours and diligently. All that the power plant construction had earned for Bill, the boy had turned in to help his mother. But Mr. Grier, busy at house building and doing better than at most other times, was able to add something to *his* boy's earnings, so that Gus could capitalize the undertaking, which he was eager to do.

The layout of the radio receiver outfits to be built alike were put at first on paper, full size; plan, side and end elevations and tracings were made of the same transferred to heavy manila paper. These were to be placed on the varnished panels, so that holes could be bored through paper and panel, thus insuring perfect spacing and arrangement. Sketches, also, were made of all details.

The audion tubes, storage batteries and telephone receivers had been purchased in the city. Almost all the other parts were made by the boys out of carefully selected materials. The amplifiers consisted of iron core transformers comprising several stages of radio frequency. The variometers were wound of 22-gauge wire. Loose couplers were used instead of the ordinary tuning coil. The switch arms, pivoting shafts and attachments for same, the contact points and binding posts were home-made. A potentiometer puzzled them most, both the making and the application, but they mastered this rather intricate mechanism, as they did the other parts.

Wayne Whipple and S. F. Aaron

In this labor, with everything at hand and a definite object in view, no boys ever were happier, nor more profitably employed, considering the influence upon their characters and future accomplishments. How true it is that they who possess worthy hobbies, especially those governed by the desire for construction and the inventive tendency, are getting altogether the most out of life and are giving the best of themselves!

The work progressed steadily - not too hastily, but most satisfactorily. Leaving at supper time, Bill's eyes would sparkle as he talked over their efforts for that day, and quiet Gus would listen with nods and make remarks of appreciation now and then.

"The way we've made that panel, Gus, with those end cleats doweled on and the shellacking of both sides - it'll never warp. I'm proud of that and it was mostly your idea."

"No, yours. I would have grooved the wood and used a tongue, but the dowels are firmer."

"A tongue would have been all right."

"But, dear boy, the dowels were easier to put in."

"Oh, well, it's done now. To-morrow we'll begin the mounting and wiring. Then for the aerial!"

But that very to-morrow brought with it the hardest blow the boys had yet had to face. Full of high spirits, they walked the half mile out to the Hooper place and found the garage a mass of blackened ruins. It had caught fire, quite mysteriously, toward morning, and the gardener and chauffeur, roused by the crackling flames, had worked like beavers but with only time to push out the two automobiles; they could save nothing else.

The Hoopers had just risen from breakfast when the boys arrived; at once Grace came out, and her expressions of regret were such as to imply that the family had lost nothing, the boys being the only sufferers. And it *was* a bit staggering - all their work and machinery and tools and plans utterly ruined - the lathe and drill a heap of twisted iron. It was with a rueful face that Bill surveyed the catastrophe.

"Never mind, Billy," said Grace, detecting evidence of moisture in his eyes; but she went over to smiling Gus and gazed at him in wonder. "Don't you care?" she asked.

"You bet I care; mostly on Bill's account, though. He had set his heart mighty strong on this. I'm sorry about your loss, too."

"Oh, never mind that! Dad is 'phoning now for carpenters and his builder. He'll be out in a minute."

Out he did come, with a shout of greeting; he, too, had sensed that the real regrets would be with them.

"It'll be all right, me lads!" he shouted. "Herring'll be here on the next train, with a bunch o' men, an' I'll git your dad, Gus, too. Must have this building up just like it was in ten days. An' now count up just what you lads have lost; the hull sum total, b'jinks! I'm goin' to be the insurance comp'ny in this deal."

"The insurance company!" Bill exclaimed and Gus stared.

"Sure. Goin' to make up your loss an' then some. I'm a heap int'rested in this Eddy's son business, ain't I? Think I ain't wantin' to see that there contraption that hears a hunderd miles off? Get busy an' give me the expense. We've got to git a-goin'."

"But, Mr. Hooper, our loss isn't yours and you have got enough to -"

"Don't talk; figger! I'm runnin' this loss business. Don't want to make me mad; eh? Git at it an' hurry up!" He turned and walked away. Grace followed in a moment, but over her shoulder remarked to the wondering boys:

"Do as Dad says if you want to keep our friendship. Dad isn't any sort of a piker, - you know that."

The insistency was too direct; "the queen's wish was a command." The boys would have to comply and they could get square with their good friends in the end. So at it they went, Bill with pad and pencil, Gus calling out the items as his eye or his memory gleaned them from the hard-looking objects in the burned mass as he raked it over. Presently Grace came out again.

"Dad wants the list and the amount," she said. "He's got to go to the city with Mr. Herring."

Bill handed over his pad and she was gone, to return as quickly in a few minutes.

"Here is an order on the bank; you can draw the cash as you need it. You can start working in the stable loft; then bring your stuff over. There will be a watchman on the grounds from to-night, so don't worry about any more fires. I must go help get Dad off."

Once more she retreated; again she stopped to say something, as an afterthought, over her shoulder:

"And, boys, won't you let Skeets and me help you some? Skeets will be here again next week and I love to tinker and contrive and make all sorts of things; it'll be fun to see the radio receiver grow."

"Sure, you can," said Gus; and Bill nodded, adding: "We have only a limited time now, and any help will count a lot."

Going down to the bank, Bill again outlined the work in detail, suggesting the purchases of even better machinery and tools, of only the best grades of materials. There must be another trip to the city, the most strenuous part of the work.

"We'll get it through on time, I guess," said Bill.

"I'm not thinking so much of that as about how that fire started," said Gus.

"It couldn't have been any of our chemicals, could it?"

"Chem - ? My eye! Don't you know, old chap? I'll bet Mr. Hooper and Grace have the correct suspicion."

"More crooked business? You don't mean -"

"Sure, I do! Thad, of course. And, Bill, we're going to get him, sooner or later. Mr. Hooper won't want to stand this sort of thing forever. I've got a hunch that we're not through with that game yet."

# CHAPTER XX

## "TO LABOR AND TO WAIT"

It was truly astonishing what well organized labor could do under intelligent direction; the boys had a fine example of this before them and a fine lesson in the accomplishment. The new garage grew into a new and somewhat larger building, on the site of the old, almost over night. There were three eight-hour shifts of men and two foremen, with the supervising architect and Mr. Grier apparently always on the job. As soon as the second floor was laid, the roof on and the sheathing in place, Bill and Gus moved in. The men gave them every aid and Mr. Grier gave special attention to building their benches, trusses, a drawing-board stand, shelving and tool chests. Then, how those new radio receivers did come on!

Grace and Skeets were given little odd jobs during the very few hours of their insistent helping. They varnished, polished, oiled, cleaned copper wire, unpacked material, even swept up the *debris* left by the carpenters; at least, they did until Skeets managed to fall headlong down about one-half of the unfinished stairway and to sprain her ankle. Then Grace's loyalty compelled her attention to her friend.

Mr. Hooper breezed in from time to time, but never to take a hand; to do so would have seemed quite out of place, though the old gentleman laughingly made an excuse for this:

"Lads, I ain't no tinker man; never was. Drivin' a pesky nail's a huckleberry above my persimmon. Cattle is all I know, an' I kin still learn about them, I reckon. But I know what I kin see an' hear an', b'jinks, I'm still doubtin' I'm ever goin' to hear that there Eddy's son do this talkin'. But get busy, lads; get busy!"

"Oh, fudge, Dad! Can't you see they're dreadfully busy? You can't hurry them one bit faster." Grace was ever just.

"No," said Skeets, who had borrowed Bill's crutch to get into the shop for a little while. "No, Mr. Hooper; if they were to stay up all night, go without eats and work twenty-five hours a day they couldn't do any -" And just then the end of the too-much inclined crutch skated outward and the habitually unfortunate girl dropped kerplunk on the floor. Gus and Grace picked her up. She was not hurt by her fall. Her very plumpness had saved her.

"For goodness' sake, Skeets, are you ever going to get the habit of keeping yourself upright?" asked Grace, who laughed harder than the others, except Skeets herself; the stout girl generally got the utmost enjoyment out of her own troubles.

Quiet restored, Mr. Hooper returned to his subject.

"I reckon you lads, when you git this thing made that's goin' to hoodoo the air, will be startin' in an' tryin' somethin' else; eh?" he ventured, grinning.

"Later, perhaps, but not just yet," Bill replied. "Not until we can manage to learn a lot more, Gus and I. Mr. Grier says that the competition of brains nowadays is a lot sharper than it was in Edison's young days, and even he had to study and work a lot before he really did any big inventing. Professor Gray says that a technical education is best for anyone who is going to do things, though it is a long way from making a fellow perfect and must be followed up by hard practice."

"And we can wait, I guess," put in Gus.

"Until we can manage in some way to scrape together enough cash to buy books and get apparatus for experiments and go on with our schooling."

"We want more physics and especially electricity," said Gus.

"And other knowledge as well, along with that," Bill amended.

"I reckon you fellers is right," said Mr. Hooper, "but I don't know anything about it. I quit school when I was eleven, but that ain't sayin' I don't miss it. If I had an eddication now, like you lads is goin' to git, er like the Perfesser has, I'd give more'n half what I own. Boys that think they're smart to quit school an' go to work is natchal fools. A feller may git along an' make money, but he'd make a heap more an' be a heap happier, 'long of everything else, if he'd got a schoolin'. An' any boy that's got real sand in his gizzard can buckle down to books an' get a schoolin', even if he don't like it. What I'm a learnin' nowadays makes me know that a feller can make any old study int'restin' if he jes' sets down an' looks at it the right way."

"That's what Gus and I think. There are studies we don't like very much, but we can make ourselves like them for we've got to know a lot about them."

"Grammar, for instance," said Gus.

"Sure. It is tiresome stuff, learning a lot of rules that work only half. But if a fellow is going to be anybody and wants to stand in with people, he's got to know how to talk correctly and write, too." Bill's logic was sound.

"Daddy should have had a drilling in grammar," commented Grace, laughing.

"Oh, you!" blurted Skeets. "Mr. Hooper can talk so that people understand him - and when you *do* talk," she turned to the old gentleman, "I notice folks are glad to listen, and so is Grace."

"But, my dear," protested the subject of criticism, "they'd listen better an' grin less if I didn't sling words about like one o' these here Eye-talians shovelin' dirt."

"You just keep a-shovelin', Mr. Hooper, your own way," said Bill, "and if we catch anybody even daring to grin at you, why, I'll have Gus land on them with his famous grapple!"

Mr. Hooper threw back his coat, thrust his thumbs into the armholes of his big, white vest and swelled out his chest.

"Now, listen to that! An' this from a lad who ain't got a thing to expect from me an' ain't had as much as he's a-givin' me, either - an' knows it. But that's nothin' else but Simon pure frien'ship, I take it. An' Gus, here, him an' Bill, they think about alike; eh, Gus?" Gus nodded and the old gentleman continued, addressing his remarks to his daughter and Skeets:

"Now, if I know anything at all about anything at all I know what I'm goin' to do. I ain't got no eddication, but that ain't goin' to keep me from seein' some others git it. You Gracie, fer one, an' you, too, Skeeter, if your old daddy'll let you come an' go to school with Gracie. But that ain't all; if you lads kin git ol' Eddy's son out o' the air on this contraption you're makin' an' hear him talk fer sure, I'm goin' to see to it that you kin git all the tec - tec - what you call it? - eddication there is goin' an' I'm goin' to put Perfesser Gray wise on that, too, soon's he comes back. No - don't you say a word now. I know what I'm a-doin'." With that the old gentleman turned and marched out of the shop. But at the bottom of the garage steps he called back:

"Say, boys, I gotta go away fer a couple o' weeks, or mebbe three. Push it right along an' mebbe you'll be hearin' from old man Eddy's son when I git back!"

# CHAPTER XXI

## EARLY STRUGGLES

The receiving outfits were completed; the aerials had been put up, one installed at the garage, the other at the mansion. Grace naturally had all, the say about placing the one in her home. The aerial, of four wires, each thirty feet long and parallel, were attached equi-distant, and at each end to springy pieces of ash ten feet long, these being insulators in part and sustained by spiral spring cables, each divided by a glass insulator block, the extended cables being fastened to a maple tree and the house chimney. The ground wire went down the side of the house beside a drain pipe.

The house receiver, in a cabinet that had cost the boys much painstaking labor, was set by a window and, after Grace and Skeets had been instructed how to tune the instrument to varying wave lengths, they and good Mrs. Hooper enjoyed many delightful periods of listening in, all zealously consulting the published programs from the great broadcasting stations.

The other outfit made by the boys, which, except the elaborate box and stand, was an exact duplicate of the Hooper receiver, was taken to the Brown cottage. Gus insisted that Bill had the best right to it, and as the Griers and Mrs. Brown had long been the best of friends and lived almost next door to each other, all the members of the carpenter's family would be welcome to listen in whenever they wanted to. The little evening gatherings at certain times for this purpose were both mirthful and delightful.

The boys' aerial was a three-wire affair, stretching forty feet, and erected in much the same way as that at the Hooper house, except that one mast had to be put up as high as the gable end of the cottage, which was the other support, thirty-five feet high.

Then, when the announcement was made that the talks on Edison were to be repeated, Bill and Gus told the class and others of their friends, so the Hoopers came also, the merry crowd filling the Brown living-room. Mr. Hooper's absence was noted and regretted from the first, as his eagerness "to be shown" was well known to them all.

The first lectures concerning Edison's boyhood were repeated. The second and third talks were each better attended than the preceding ones. Cora, Dot, Skeets and two other girls occupied the front row; Ted Bissell and Terry Watkins were present. Bill presided with much dignity, most carefully tuning in, making the announcements, then becoming the most interested listener, the theme being ever dear to him.

On the occasion of the third lecture, Bill said:

"Now, then, classmates and other folks, this is a new one to all of us. The last was where we left off in June on the Professor's receiver. You can just bet this is going to be a pippin. First off, though, is a violin solo by - by - oh, I forget his name, - and may it be short and sweet!"

After the music, the now well-known voice came from the horn:

"This is the third talk on the career and accomplishments of Thomas Alva Edison:

"In a little while young Edison began to get tired of the humdrum life of a telegraph operator in Boston. As I have told you, after the vote-recorder, he had invented a stock ticker and started a quotation service in Boston. He opened operations from a room over the Gold Exchange with thirty to forty subscribers.

"He also engaged in putting up private lines, upon which he used an alphabetical dial instrument for telegraphing between business establishments, a forerunner of modern telephony. This instrument was very simple and practical, and any one could work it after a few minutes' explanation.

"The inventor has described an accident he suffered and its effect on him:

"'In the laboratory,' he says, 'I had a large induction coil. One day I got hold of both electrodes of this coil, and it clinched my hands on them so that I could not let go!

"'The battery was on a shelf. The only way I could get free was to back off and pull the coil, so that the battery wires would pull the cells off the shelf and thus break the circuit. I shut my eyes and pulled, but the nitric acid splashed all over my face and ran down my back.

"'I rushed to a sink, which was only half big enough, and got in as well as I could, and wiggled around for several minutes to let the water dilute the acid and stop the pain. My face and back were streaked with yellow; the skin was thoroughly oxidized.

"'I did not go on the street by daylight for two weeks, as the appearance of my face was dreadful. The skin, however, peeled off, and new skin replaced it without any damage.'

"The young inventor went to New York City to seek better fortunes. First he tried to sell his stock printer and failed in the effort. Then he returned to Boston and got up a duplex telegraph - for sending two messages at once over one wire. He tried to demonstrate it between Rochester and New York City.

After a week's trial, his test did not work, partly because of the inefficiency of his assistant.

"He had run in debt eight hundred dollars to build this duplex apparatus. His other inventions had cost considerable money to make, and he had failed to sell them. So his books, apparatus and other belongings were left in Boston, and when he returned to New York he arrived there with but a few cents in his pocket. He was very hungry. He walked the streets in the early morning looking for breakfast but with so little money left that he did not wish to spend it.

"Passing a wholesale tea house, he saw a man testing tea by tasting it. The young inventor asked the 'taster' for some of the tea. The man smiled and held out a cup of the fragrant drink. That tea was Thomas A. Edison's first breakfast in New York City.

"He walked back and forth hunting for a telegraph operator he had known, but that young man was also out of work. When Edison finally found him, all his friend could do was to lend him a dollar!

"By this time Edison was nearly starved. With such limited resources he gave solemn thought to what he should select that would be most satisfying. He decided to buy apple dumplings and coffee, and in telling afterward of his first real 'eats' in New York, Mr. Edison said he never had anything that tasted so good.

"Just as young Ben Franklin, on arriving in New York City from Boston, looked for a job in a printing office, the youthful modern inventor applied for work in a telegraph office there. As there was no vacancy and he needed the rest of his borrowed dollar for meals, Edison found lodging in the battery room of the Gold Indicator Company.

"It was four years after the Civil War and, besides there being much unemployment, the fluctuations in the value of gold, as compared with the paper currency of that day, made it necessary to have gold 'indicators' something like the tickers from the Stock Exchange to-day. Dr. Laws, presiding officer of the Gold Exchange, had recently invented a system of gold indicators, which were placed in brokers' offices and operated from the Gold Exchange.

"When Edison got permission to spend the night in the battery room of this company, there were about three hundred of these instruments operating in offices in all directions in lower New York City.

"On the third day after his arrival, while sitting in this office, the complicated instrument sending quotations out on all the lines made a very loud noise, and came to a sudden stop with a crash. Within two minutes over three hundred boys - one from every broker's office in the street - rushed upstairs and crowded the long aisle and office where there was hardly room for one-third that number, each yelling that a certain broker's wire was out of order, and that it must be fixed at once.

"It was pandemonium, and the manager got so wild that he lost all control of himself. Edison went to the indicator, and as he had already studied it thoroughly, he knew right where the trouble was. He went right out to see the man in charge, and found Dr. Laws there also - the most excited man of all!

"The Doctor demanded to know what caused all the trouble, but his man stood there, staring and dumb. As soon as Edison could get Laws' attention he told him he knew what the matter was.

"'Fix it! Fix it! and be quick about it!' Dr. Laws shouted.

"Edison went right to work and in two hours had everything in running order. Dr. Laws came in to ask the inventor's name and what he was doing. When told, he asked the young man to call on him in his office the next day. Edison did so and Laws said he had decided to place Edison in charge of the entire plant at a salary of three hundred dollars a month!

"This was such a big jump from any wages he had ever received that it quite paralyzed the youthful inventor. He felt that it was too much to last long, but he made up his mind he would do his best to earn that salary if he had to work twenty hours a day. He kept that job, making improvements and devising other stock tickers, until the Gold and Stock Telegraph Company consolidated with the Gold Indicator Company."

# CHAPTER XXII

## FAME AND FORTUNE

"At twenty-two," the lecturer continued, "while Edison was with the Gold and Stock Telegraph Company, he often heard Jay Gould and 'Jim' Fisk, the great Wall Street operators of that day, talk over the money market. At night he ate his lunches in the coffee-house in Printing House Square, where he used to meet Henry J. Raymond, founder of *The New York Times*, Horace Greeley of the *Tribune* and James Gordon Bennett of the *Herald*, the greatest trio of journalists in the world. One of the most memorable remarks made by a frequenter of this night lunch, as recorded by Mr. Edison was:

"'This is a great place; a plate of cakes, a cup of coffee, and a Russian bath, all for ten cents!'

"The so-called bath was on account of the heat of the crowded room.

"Mr. Edison tells this story of the terrible panic in Wall Street, in September, 1869, brought on chiefly by the attempt of Jay Gould and his associates to corner the gold market:

"'On Black Friday we had a rather exciting time with our indicators. The Gould and Fisk crowd had cornered the gold and had run up the quotations faster than the indicator could record them. In the morning it was quoting 150 premium while Gould's agents were bidding 165 for five millions or less.

"'There was intense excitement. Broad and other streets in the Wall Street district were crammed with crazy crowds. In the midst of the excitement, Speyer, another large operator, became so insane that it took five men to hold him. I sat on the roof of a Western Union booth and watched the surging multitudes.

"'A Western Union man I knew came up and said to me: "Shake hands, Edison. We're all right. We haven't got a cent to lose."'

"After the company with which our young inventor was connected had sold out its inventions and improvements to the Gold and Stock Telegraph Company, Mr. Edison produced a machine to print gold quotations instead of merely indicating them. The attention of the president of the Gold and Stock Company was attracted to the success of the wonderful young inventor.

"Edison had produced quite a number of inventions. One of these was the special ticker which was used many years in other large cities, because it was so simple that it could be operated by men less expert than the operators in New York. It was used also on the London Stock Exchange.

"After he had gotten up a good many inventions and taken out patents for them, the president of the big company came to see him and was shown a simple device to regulate tickers that had been printing figures wrong. This thing saved a good deal of labor to a large number of men, and prevented trouble for the broker himself. It impressed the president so much that he invited Edison into his private office and said, in a stage whisper:

"'Young man, I would like to settle with you for your inventions here. How much do you want for them?"

"Edison had thought it all over and had come to the conclusion that, on account of the hard night-and-day work he had been doing, he really ought to have five thousand dollars, but he would be glad to settle for three thousand, if they thought five thousand was too much. But when asked point-blank, he hadn't the courage to name either sum - thousands looked large to him then - so he hesitated a bit and said:

"'Well, General, suppose *you* make *me* an offer.'

"'All right,' said the president. 'How would forty thousand dollars strike you?'

"Young Edison came as near fainting then as he ever did in his life. He was afraid the 'General' would hear his heart thump, but he said quietly that he thought that amount was just about right. A contract was drawn up which Edison signed without reading.

"Forty thousand dollars was written in the first check Thomas A. Edison ever received. With throbbing heart and trembling fingers he took it to the bank and handed it in to the paying teller, who looked at it disapprovingly and passed it back, saying something the young inventor could not hear because of his deafness. Thinking he had been cheated, Edison went out of the bank, as he said, 'to let the cold sweat evaporate.'

"Then he hurried back to the president and demanded to know what it all meant. The president and his secretary laughed at the green youth's needless fears and explained that the teller had probably told him to write his name on the back of the check. They not only showed him how to endorse it, but sent a clerk to the bank to identify him - because of the large amount of money to be paid over.

"Just for a joke on the 'jay,' the teller gave him the whole forty thousand dollars in ten- and twenty-dollar bills. Edison gravely stowed away the money till he had filled all his pockets including those in his overcoat. He sat up all night in his room in Newark, in fear and trembling, lest he be robbed. The president laughed next day but said that joke had gone far enough; then he showed Thomas A. Edison how to open his first bank account."

Again the lecturer's voice ceased to be heard; again another voice announced that the fourth talk would be given on a certain date a few days later. A negro song with banjo accompaniment followed and the radio entertainment was over.

Everyone was talking, laughing and voicing pleasure in the increasingly wonderful demonstration of getting sounds out of the air, from hundreds of miles away. Only Gus and Bill remained and the two - as Billy always referred to their confabs - went into "executive session." This radio receiver was altogether absorbing, much too attractive to let alone easily. The boys were proud of their very successful construction and they could neither forget that fact, nor pass up the delight of listening in.

This time Gus had the first inspiration. Billy often thought how, sometimes strangely or by chance or correct steering, his chum seemed to grasp the deeper matters of detection. Gus eagerly acknowledged Bill as possessing a genius for mechanical construction and invention, without which the comrades would get nowhere in such efforts, even admitting Gus's skill and cleverness with tools. But when it came to having hunches and good luck concerning matters of human mystery, Gus was the king pin.

"I'm going to see what else we can get from near or far," Gus said, detaching the horn and using the head clamp with its two ear 'phones which had been added to the set. He sat down and began moving the switch arms, one from contact to contact, the other throughout the entire range of its contacts at each movement of the first, and proceeding thus slowly for some minutes.

Bill had turned to the study of his Morse code, which the boys had taken up and pursued at every opportunity during the building of the radio sets. Gus, however, was less familiar with the dots and dashes. A whisper, as though Gus were afraid the sound of his voice would disturb the electric waves, suddenly switched Bill's attention.

"Two dots, three dots, two dots, one dash, one dot and dash, one dot, one dash and two dots, same, dot, dash, dot, two dots, two dashes and dot, four dots, one dash, two dots, two dashes, two dots." A pause. Gus had whispered each signal to Bill; then he asked: "What do you make it?"

"I make it: 'Is it all right, then?' They have been talking some time, I guess," said Bill; and added: "That's a good way to pick up and wrestle with the code; it's dandy practice and we want -"

"Wait, pal, wait!" gasped Gus, bending forward again.

Words came now, instead of the code. It was evident that the person giving them out had sought authority for so doing from headquarters.

Gus heard:

"This is to whom it may concern: Five hundred dollars' reward is to be paid for information leading to the arrest of a party who last night broke into the home of Nathan R. Hallowell. After deliberately and, without apparent cause, shooting and badly wounding Mrs. Hallowell and striking down an old servant woman, he stole several hundred dollars' worth of jewels and silverware. Both the servant, who kept her wits about her, and Mrs. Hallowell, who is now out of danger, have described the assailant. He is about eighteen, of medium height, slender, dark complexioned, one eye noticeably smaller than the other, nose long and pointed, has a nervous habit of twitching his shoulder. He wore a light brown suit and a gray cap. Send all information, or broadcast same to Police Headquarters, Willstown. Immediate detention of any reasonable suspect is recommended."

Gus wheeled about.

"Bill, it's Thad! Description hits him exactly and there's five hundred reward. He's done a house-breaking stunt and tried to kill two people and I don't believe they've got him yet. Mr. Hooper wouldn't want us to keep quiet on this; would he?"

"It might be a good idea to talk to Mrs. Hooper and Grace about it before you inform on Thad," Bill said.

"I'll do that," Gus agreed and was off. In half an hour he was back again.

"I saw them, late as it was. Grace and Skeets were playing crokinole and Mrs. Hooper came down. And, what do you think? Mr. Hooper wrote that Thad had forged his name on a check for several hundred dollars and got away with it and, even if he did still want to shield Thad, the law wouldn't let him. Grace says Thad ought to be caught and punished and that her father will want it done."

"But Gus, even if you got Willstown on the long distance 'phone, how would that help to -"

"We'll get them later; after we have located Thad."

"Oh, Gus, do you think Ben Shultz was dreaming?"

"When he said he saw Thad out there in the barren ground woods by the old cabin? Not a bit of it! It's the last place they'd ever think of looking for him - right on his uncle's place. Thad is pretty keen in some ways. But I doubt if he'll stay there long. He'll be pulling out for the mountains. There's a late moon to-night, you see."

"I wish I could go with you; this old leg -"

"Never mind now; don't worry. I'll take Bennie Shultz and make him messenger. If Thad's there you can get down to the drug store and call Willstown. That'll make our case sure. By cracky, old scout, five hundred! We can -"

"Chickens, old man; chickens. Hatch 'em first. But you will, I'll bet, and it will be yours; not -"

"What are you talking about? Ours! It's as much your job as mine. Divy-divy, half n'half, fifty-fifty. Well, I'm off."

# CHAPTER XXIII

## JUSTICE

"Now then, Bennie," whispered Gus, "beat it on the q.t. Then streak it for Bill's house. He'll be watching for you. Tell him our man is here and probably getting ready to light out. You needn't come back; I'm only going to spot this bird and find out where he goes, if I can. You'll get well paid for this, kid."

The two boys were lying on the sandy ground among young cedars, and watching the little cabin not fifty yards distant. Out of this crude shack had come the sole occupant, to stand and gaze about him for a minute, lifting his face to the moon. Gus could plainly distinguish the gray cap, the slender build of the youth; he recognized the walk, a certain manner of standing, and once he plainly caught that upward shift of the shoulder. Then Gus gave his orders to Bennie, knowing that they would be carried out with precision, for the little fellow, almost a waif and lacking proper influences, would have nearly laid down his life for Gus after the athlete had very deservedly whipped two town bullies that were making life miserable for him. Moreover, the youngster wanted to be like Gus and Bill, in the matter of mentality, and a promise of reward meant money with which he could buy books.

Left alone, Gus crept nearer the cabin. He could be reasonably sure of himself, but not of Bennie, who might crack a stick or sneeze. Some low cedars grew on the slope above the cabin; Gus took advantage of these and got within about forty feet of the shack. Then he lay watching for fully an hour, there being no sign of the inmate. But after what had seemed to Gus almost half the night, out came the suspect, stood a moment as before and started off; it could be seen that he carried a small pack and a heavy stick in his hands.

Then Gus was taken by surprise; even his ready intuition failed him. He had made up his mind that he was in for a long hike to the not too distant mountains and that over this ground the work of keeping the other fellow in sight and of keeping out of sight himself was going to mean constant vigilance and keen stalking. But the midnight prowler swung around the cabin and with long, certain strides headed straight for the Hooper mansion.

This was easier going for Gus than the open road toward the mountains would have been; there was plenty of growth - long grass, trees and bushes - to keep between him and the other who never tried to seek shelter, nor hardly once looked behind him until the end of the broad driveway was reached.

Gus knew the watchman must be about, though possibly half asleep. He also believed that the suspected youth, by the way he advanced, must know the ways of the watchman. Roger, the big Saint Bernard, let out a booming roar and came bounding down the driveway; the fellow spoke to him and that was all there was to that. Gus stayed well behind, fearing the friendly beast might come to him also and thus give his presence away, but Roger was evidently coaxed to remain with the first comer.

The big house stood silent, bathed in the moonlight; there was no sign of anyone about, other than the miscreant who stood now in the shadow, surveying the place. Presently he put down his pack, went to a window and, quick and silent as an expert burglar, jimmied the sash. There was only one sudden, sharp snap of the breaking sash bolt and in a moment the fellow had vanished within the darkness and Gus distinguished only the occasional flash of a pocket torch inside.

There was but one thing to do, and that as quickly as possible. The dog had gone around to lie again on the front veranda. Gus made a bolt for the rear of the grounds, reached the garage, found an open door, began softly to push it open and suddenly found himself staring into the muzzle of a revolver that protruded from the blackness beyond.

"Don't shoot! I'm Gus Grier, Mr. Watchman." The boy was conscious of a certain unsteadiness in his own voice.

"Oh! An' phwat air yes doin' here?"

"Talk low," said Gus, "but listen first: There's a burglar in the house. I spotted him some time ago, followed him and saw him get through the dining-room window. Move fast and he's yours!"

Pat moved fast. He recognized that he had not been up to his duty so far and he meant to make amends. With Gus following, the boy's nerves on edge with the possibility that the housebreaker would shoot, the Irishman, who was no coward, reached the house, entered the basement, flooded the house with light, alarmed the inmates and in a few minutes had every avenue of escape guarded, the chauffeur, butler and gardener coming on the scene, all half dressed and armed.

What followed needs little telling. Hardly had the men decided to search the house before the sound of a rapidly approaching motor horn was heard and from the quickly checked car two men leaped out, the constable and a deputy from the town - and then Bill Brown! The illuminated house had stopped their course. The search revealed Thad cowering in a closet, all the fight gone out of him. Grace and Skeets were not even awakened; Mrs. Hooper did not leave her room.

As the constable turned a light on the handcuffed prisoner he remarked: "That's the chap all right. Description fits. He'll bring that five hundred all right."

"A reward; is it?" said the watchman. "An' don't ye fergit who gits it. Not me, ner you, Constable, but the bye here." He laid his hand on Gus's shoulder. The constable laughed:

"Oh, you're slow, Pat. We all know that. The kid and his pal, that young edition of Edison by the name of Billy Brown, got the thing cinched over their radio. We didn't know that the description that Willstown sent out fitted Mr. Hooper's own nephew."

And so with relief, mixed with regret for Mr. Hooper's sake, Gus and Bill saw a sulky and rebellious Thad vanish into the night and out of their immediate affairs.

## CHAPTER XXIV

## GENIUS IS OFTEN ERRATIC

The fourth radio talk on the life, character and accomplishments of the world's foremost inventor proved to be the most interesting of the series. Fairview had heard of these entertainments and so many people had asked Bill and Gus if they might attend, the boys became aware that the modest little living-room of the Brown home would not hold half of them. They, therefore, decided to let the radio be heard in the town hall, if a few citizens would pay the rent for the evening.

This was readily arranged, but when the suggestion was made that an admission be charged, the boys refused. This was their treat all round, even to transferring their aerial to the hall between its cupola and a mast at the other end of the roof, put up by the ever willing Mr. Grier who could not do too much to further the boys' interests.

Early in the evening the hall was filled to overflowing, and ushers were appointed to seat the crowd. Naturally there was much chattering and scraping of feet until suddenly a strain of music, an orchestral selection, began to come out of the horn and there was instant quiet. After its conclusion came the voice:

"This is our last lecture on Edison. Following this will be given a series on Marconi, the inventor of the wireless.

"As I have told you, Mr. Thomas Alva Edison's leap to fortune was sudden and spectacular, as have been most of his accomplishments since. Those who do really great things along the lines of physical improvement, or concerning the inception of large enterprises are apt to startle the public and to surprise thoughtful people almost as though some impossible thing had been achieved.

"From a mere salaried operator to forty thousand dollars in a lump sum for expert work was quite a jump.

"The forty thousand dollars, however, did not turn Mr. Edison's head as has been the effect of sudden wealth on many a good-sized but smaller minded man.

"He used it as a fund to start a plant and hire expert men to experiment and work out the inventions which came to him so fast in his ceaseless work and study. He could get along with as little sleep as Napoleon is said to have required when a mighty battle was on. Edison could lie down on a settee or table and sleep just as the Little Corporal did even while cannon were booming all around him.

"There was something Napoleonic, also, about Edison's intensity of application and his masterfulness in his gigantic undertakings. If genius is the ability to take great pains, Thomas A. Edison is the greatest genius in the world to-day - if not in all history.

"Sometimes, as Napoleon did with his chief generals before a decisive engagement, Edison would shut himself up with his confidential coworkers. Sometimes he and they would neither eat nor sleep till they had fought out a problem of greater importance to the world than even Napoleon's crossing the Alps or the decisive battle of Austerlitz. But, though he began to work on a large scale, young Edison's financial facilities were of the crudest and simplest.

"Almost all of his men were on piece-work, and he allowed

them to make good salaries. He never cut them down, although their pay was very high as they became more and more expert.

"Instead of *books* he kept *hooks* - two of them. All the bills he owed he jabbed on one hook, and stuck mems of what was due him on the other. If he had no tickers ready to deliver when an account came due, he gave his note for the amount required.

"Then as one bill after another fell due, a bank messenger came with a notice of protest pinned to the note, demanding a dollar and a quarter extra for protest fees besides principal and interest. Whereupon he would go to New York and borrow more funds, or pay the note on the spot if he happened to have money enough on hand. He kept up this expensive way of doing business for two years, but his credit was perfectly good. Every dealer he patronized was glad to furnish him with what he wanted, and some expressed admiration for his new method of paying bills.

"But, to save his own time, Edison had to hire a bookkeeper whose inefficiency made him regret for a while the change in his way of doing business. He tells of one of his experiences with this accountant:

"'After the first three months I told him to go through his books and see how much we had made.

"Three thousand dollars!" he told me after studying a while. So, to celebrate this, I gave a dinner to several of the staff.

"'Two days after that he came to tell me he had made a big mistake, for we had *lost* five hundred dollars. Several days later he came round again and tried to prove to me that we had made seven thousand dollars in the three months!'

"This was so disconcerting that the inventor decided to change bookkeepers, but he never 'counted his chickens before they were hatched.' In other words, he did not believe that he had made anything till he had paid all his bills and had his money safe in the bank.

"Mr. Edison once made the remark that when Jay Gould got possession of the Western Union Telegraph Company, no further progress in telegraphy was possible, because Gould took no pride in building up. All he cared for was money, only money.

"The opposite was true of Edison. While he had decided to invent only that which was of commercial value, it was not on account of the money but because that which millions of people will buy is of the greatest value to the world.

"After he stopped telegraphing, Edison turned his mind to many inventions. It is not generally known that the first successful, widely sold typewriter was perfected by him.

"This typewriter proved a difficult thing to make commercial. The alignment of the letters was very bad. One letter would be one-sixteenth of an inch above the others, and all the letters wanted to wander out of line. He worked on it till the machine gave fair results. The typewriter he got into commercial shape is now known as the Remington.

"It is not hard to understand that Mr. Edison invented the American District Messenger call-box system, which has been superseded by the telephone, but very few people know when they are eating caramels and other sticky confectionery that wax or paraffin paper was invented by Edison. Also the tasimeter, an instrument so delicate that it measures the heat of the most distant star, Arcturus. One of the few vacations Mr. Edison allowed himself was when he traveled to the Rocky Mountains to witness a total eclipse of the sun and experiment on certain stars with his tasimeter, and this very clearly shows that Mr. Edison is as much interested in the advancement of science as in matters purely commercial."

# CHAPTER XXV

## THE GENIUS OF THE AGE

"I want to tell you something more about the personal side of this great man," continued the voice from the horn.

"One of the striking things about Thomas Alva Edison is his gameness. In this respect he has been greater than Napoleon, who was not always a 'good loser,' for he had come to regard himself as bound to win, whether or no; so when everything went against him, he expressed himself by kicking against Fate. But when Edison saw the hard work of nine years which had cost him two million dollars vanish one night in a sudden storm, he only laughed and said, 'I never took much stock in spilt milk.'

"When his laboratories were burned or he suffered great reverses, Edison considered them merely the fortunes of war. In this respect he was most like General Washington, who, though losing more battles than he gained, learned to 'snatch victory from the jaws of defeat,' and win immortal success.

"Some of Edison's discoveries were dramatic and amusing. During his telephone experiments he learned the power of a diaphragm to take up sound vibrations, and he had made a little toy that, when you talked into the funnel, would start a paper man sawing wood. Then he came to the conclusion that if he could record the movements of the diaphragm well enough he could cause such records to reproduce the

Wayne Whipple and S. F. Aaron

movements imparted to them by the human voice.

"But in place of using a disk, he got up a small machine with a cylinder provided with grooves around the surface. Over this some tinfoil was to be placed and he gave it to an assistant to construct. Edison had but little faith that it would work, but he said he wanted to get up a machine that would 'talk back.' The assistant thought it was ridiculous to expect such a thing, but he went ahead and followed the directions given him. Edison has told of this:

"'When it was finished and the foil was put on, I shouted a verse of "Mary had a little lamb" into the crude little machine. Then I adjusted the reproducer, which when he began to operate it, proceeded to grind out -

"'Mary had a little lamb,
Its fleece was white as snow,
And everywhere that Mary went,
The lamb was sure to go'

"with the very quality and tones of my voice! We were never so taken back in our lives. All hands were called in to witness the phenomenon and, recovering from their astonishment, the boys joined hands and danced around me, singing and shouting in their excitement. Then each yelled something at the machine - bits of slang or slurs - and it made them roar to hear that funny little contraption 'sass back!'

"Edison has always had a saving sense of humor. Though such a driver for work - sometimes twenty hours a day seemed too short and they often worked all of twenty-four, - there was not unfrequently a jolly, prank-playing relaxation among the employees in the laboratory. If some fellow fell asleep and began snoring the others would get a record of it and play it later for the culprit or they would fix up a 'squawkophone' to outdo his racket. Most amusing was Edison's means of taking a short nap by curling up in an ordinary roll-top desk, and then turning over without falling out.

"Everybody knows Edison really invented the telephone - that is, he made it work perfectly and brought it to the greatest commercial value, so that a billion men, women and children are using it in nearly all the languages and dialects in the civilized world. But he was very careful to give Dr. Alexander Graham Bell credit for his original work on this great invention.

"When a friend on the other side of the Atlantic wired that the English had offered 'thirty thousand' for the rights to one of Edison's improvements to the telephone for that country, it was promptly accepted. When the draft came the inventor found, much to his surprise, that it was for thirty thousand *pounds* - nearly one hundred and fifty thousand dollars.

"The phonograph or talking machine has been considered one of Edison's greatest inventions, but it does not compare in importance and value with the electric incandescent burner light. This required many thousands of experiments and tests to get a filament that would burn long enough in a vacuum to make the light sufficiently cheap to compete with petroleum or gas. During all the years that he was experimenting on different metals and materials for the electric light which was yet to be, in a literal sense, the light of the world, he had men hunting in all countries for exactly the right material out of which the carbon filament now in use is made. Thousands of kinds of wood, bamboo and other vegetable substances were tried. The staff made over fifty thousand experiments in all for this one purpose. This illustrates the art and necessity of taking pains, one of Mr. Edison's greatest characteristics. The story of producing electric light would fill a big volume.

"When the proper filament was discovered and applied there was great rejoicing in the laboratory and a regular orgy of playing pranks and fun.

"The philosophers say we measure time by the succession of ideas. If this is true the time must have been longer and seemed shorter in Edison's laboratories than anywhere else.

The great inventor seldom carried a watch and seemed not to like to have clocks about.

"Soon after he was married, the story went the rounds of the press that within an hour or two after the ceremony, Edison became so engrossed with an invention that he forgot that it was his wedding day. Edison has declared this story to be untrue.

"'That's just one of the kind of yarns,' said the inventor laughing, 'that the reporters have to make up when they run short of news. It was the invention of an imaginative chap who knows I'm a little absent-minded. I never forgot that I was married.

"'But there was an incident that may have given a little color to such a story. On our wedding day a lot of stock tickers were returned to the factory and were said to need overhauling.

"'About an hour after the ceremony I was reminded of those tickers and when we got to our new home, I told my wife about them, adding that I would like to walk down to the factory a little while and see if the boys had found out what was the matter.

"'She consented and I went down and found an assistant working on the job. We both monkeyed with the machines an hour or two before we got them to rights. Then I went home.

"'My wife and I laughed at the story at first, but when we came across it about every other week, it began to get rather stale. It was one of those canards that stick, and I shall be spoken of always as the man who forgot his wife within an hour after he was married.'

"A similar yarn was told of Abraham Lincoln, which was equally false, but even more generally believed.

"Out of a multitude of labor savers and world-beaters - and

world savers, too! - to be credited to Mr. Edison, it is impossible to mention more than these:

"The quadruplex telegraph system for sending four messages - two in each direction - at the same time; the telephone carbon transmitter; the phonograph; the incandescent electric light and complete system; magnetic separator; Edison Effect now used in Radio bulbs; giant rock crushers; alkaline storage battery; motion picture camera. These are but few of Edison's inventions, but they are giving employment to over a million people and making the highest use of billions of dollars.

"With Mr. Edison's modesty it is difficult to get him to talk of the relative importance of his inventions, but he has expressed the opinion that the one of most far-reaching importance is the electric light system which includes the generation, regulation, distribution and measurement of electric current for light, heat and power. The invention he loves most is the phonograph as he is a lover of music. He has patented about twelve hundred inventions.

"Recent developments are proving that the moving picture, because of its educational and emotional appeal is the greatest of them all. It is estimated that more than one hundred millions of people go to one of these shows once every seven days, which is equivalent to every man, woman and child in the United States of America going to a movie once a week. The motion picture reaches, teaches and preaches to more people in America than all the schools, churches, books, magazines and newspapers put together, and when it teaches, it does it in a vivid way that live people like.

"Political campaigns are beginning to be carried on with the silver screen for a platform. Writers in great magazines are proving, on the authority of the Japanese themselves, that the American moving picture is re-making Japan. Another, who has studied the signs of the times, asserts that the only way to bring order out of chaos in Russia is by means of the motion picture.

"Comparisons are of times odious, but not in this case, for there is no man living, nor has there ever lived a man, except the Great Teacher, who has more greatly and generally benefited humanity or cast a stronger light upon the processes of civilization than Thomas Alva Edison."

At the close of another musical number there was a general expectation of dismissal, a shuffling of feet and a murmur of voices. This was checked suddenly by Bill. The boy had been near the receiver all the while, on the chance of being needed in case of mishap, or for a sharper "tuning in"; now he got what the others did not and rising he let out a yell:

"Everybody quiet! Something else!" and in the instant hush was heard the completion of an announcement:

" - Scouts of America, the Girl Scouts and other organizations of kindred nature, upon their urgent invitation. We are making this announcement now for the fourth and last time in the hope that it may be universally received. Mr. Edison will now probably be here within an hour from this minute. All the youth of the land who may avail themselves of radio service will please respond and listen in. In a warmly appreciative sense this must be a gala occasion."

"That's all, folks; I'm certain." Bill shouted the school yell and the class year: "Umpah, umpah, ho, ho; it's up to you, Fairview, 1922!" Then: "Bring 'em all back here, Gus."

But not one of them needed urging nor reminding. Separating themselves from the rapidly diminishing and retreating audience came Ted, Terry, Cora, Dot, Grace, with Skeets as a guest, Bert Haskell, Mary Dean, Lem Upsall, Walt Maynard, Lucy Shore and Sara Fortescue, the entire bunch eagerly attentive. They crowded around Bill and Gus and were well aware of the purpose.

"Sure, we'll all be here, I'll bet a cow!" shouted Ted.

"Dot and I could listen in on our own radio," said Cora. "We've got it finished and it works fine and dandy, Billy. We want you and Gus and everybody to come over and try it. But we'll join in with the class on this; eh, Dot?"

"Sure will," agreed Dot. "Ours is only a crystal set, but it has some improvements you boys haven't seen. Wait till we get it all done, and we'll give you a spread and a surprise."

"Say, Bill, this thing's great," Terry said. "Father is going to get me an outfit in the city and I'll pay you and Gus to set it up for -"

"Set it up yourself, you lazy thing!" said Cora.

"If you please, miss, I've got other matters -"

"All right, Terry, - see you later about it. Now, listen, hopefuls. You'll all be here, but this occasion is going to be incomplete, unless
we have a lot more on deck. We all want to get out, and scout round and fetch in every kid that wants to amount to anything at all and is big enough to understand and appreciate what's going on. And even then it won't be quite up to snuff unless -"

"I know! You want Mr. Hooper here, too!" shouted Skeets. But in trying to rise to make herself heard, she upset her chair and then sat down on the floor, jarring the building. When the shout of mirth subsided, Bill said:

"That's right. Mr. Hooper and Professor Gray. We'll have to tell them about it."

"Father wrote that he's coming home to-night," announced Grace proudly.

"Great shakes! Did he? Gus, get on the 'phone and find out!" Bill commanded. "Now, then, let's all get busy and -"

"Righto, Billy, but what will our folks think has become of us when it's so late?" Dot questioned.

"I move we go into executive session!" shouted Walt Maynard.

"Sure, and the president of the class can call a meeting," said Terry Watkins.

"It's up to you then, Billy," Cora agreed.

"I call it. Come to order and dispense with the minutes, Miss Secretary," Billy grinned at Dot. "Motion in order to send a committee to inform all the girls' parents."

"I make that motion," said Bert.

"Second it. The boys' parents can get wise by radio," asserted Ted.

"Bert and Ted appointed. Get out and get busy!" Bill was no joke as an executive. "Here's Gus. Did you get Mrs. Hooper?"

"I sure did. Mr. Hooper got home an hour ago."

"Glory!" Grace, you're driving your little runabout? I appoint Grace and Mary a committee to go and get Mr. and Mrs. Hooper here right off. No objections? Don't fail, Grace, or we'll send the entire bunch."

"We'll fetch him," laughed Grace as she and Mary hurried out.

"Now then, everybody else, including the chair, is appointed a committee to bring in every boy and girl in the town who will come. Work fast! I wonder if we could promise some eats." Bill glanced at Terry.

"Yes; tell them there'll be refreshments!" shouted the rich boy. "It'll be my treat. Bill, make me a committee of one to hive the grub. Cakes, candy, bananas and ice cream; eh?"

"Done!" declared Bill. "Go to it, with the class's blessing!"

"Yes and Heaven's best on Terry Watkins," said Cora.

In a moment the hall was empty. Twenty minutes later the Hooper party arrived and about three minutes thereafter who should appear but Professor Gray, hurried, eager, registering disappointment when he saw the empty room, then smiling as the Hoopers and Mary Dean came to greet him.

"I had hoped to find my class here," he began and was interrupted by the thump of Bill's crutch on the steps without. Forgetting his support the boy leaped, rather than limped, forward, followed more sedately by several lads and lasses he had rounded up.

"If this isn't the best thing that *ever happened*!" shouted Bill, grasping the hands of the two men held out to him. "Both of you! And you, too, Mrs. Hooper. Great! Just got back, Professor! And now we're going to get the very thing we talked about, Mr. Hooper: we're going to hear Mr. Edison's voice or that of his right-hand man, nearly three hundred miles away. The rest of the bunch will be here in a minute. I expect Gus and Ted and Cora to fetch in a few dozen besides. Hello, here's Terry with the eats."

# CHAPTER XXVI

## GOOD COUNSEL

"This quite overcomes me," said Professor Gray to Mr. Hooper. "I hurried back to invite some of my pupils to hear a message from Mr. Edison's laboratory; but trust Bill to do the thing in a monumental fashion!"

"That there lad's a reg'lar rip-snorter, Perfesser. You can't beat him. Well, now, let's set down here in the middle; eh, Mother? an' wait fer what's a-comin'. I want a chance to tell the Perfesser 'bout that there water-power plant an' what them boys done. Them's the lads, I'm a-sayin'."

But conversation was out of the question, for in came another troop of youngsters, landed by Cora, Dot and Lucy, followed a moment later by more, invited by the boys, who had joined forces in the street. The hall was half filled by an expectant and noisy throng. Of course, half of them anticipated the refreshments more eagerly than anything else. These were already, under the ministration of a young woman from the confectionery hastily engaged by Terry, now becoming evident.

Bill was beside the radio outfit, silently listening with the ear 'phones clamped to the side of his head. Suddenly he arose and shouted:

"Quiet! Silence, everybody, and listen hard!"

Out of the horn again came the well-known voice of the transmitting station official announcer:

"It gives us great pleasure to be able to broadcast very worth while messages of helpfulness and cheer to the youth of America. This occasion and opportunity was largely inspired by the Boy Scouts and the Girl Scouts and it will interest you to know that the presidents, secretaries and many of the executive officers of these splendid organizations are now here with us in person to inspire the occasion. They have asked me to express to you the hope that every Girl and Boy Scout - and I add every other self-respecting girl and boy - has access to a radio receiver and is now listening in to catch these words. I will now reproduce for you a message from one of the world's foremost citizens and greatest men, one who has brought more joy and comfort to civilized millions than any other man of his time, and therefore the greatest inventor in history; Mr. Thomas Alva Edison will now speak to the boys and girls of America through his constant associate and devoted friend, Mr. William H. Meadowcroft."

There was a slight pause. The silence in the hall was most impressive. Bill cast his eyes for a brief moment over the waiting throng. There was in the eager faces, some almost wofully serious, some half-smiling, all wide-eyed and with craning necks, a tremendous indication of an almost breathless interest. Then, from the horn came slow and measured accents in a loud voice, perhaps a trifle tremulous from a proper feeling of the gravity of the occasion, but it was perfectly distinct:

"Young people, I -"

"*That's* Bill - hello, Bill Medders - when did *you* -?"

And the startled company, staring about, saw Mr. Hooper stumbling forward in the aisle toward the trumpet.

"You win, me lads, you -"

Bill Brown could not help laughing at the impetuous honesty of his kind old friend. Pointing to the horn, and placing his hand like a shell behind his own ear, the amused boy signed to the excited old man to listen.

"The old geezer looks like 'His Master's Voice,' don't he?" came like a sneer from the background.

During the pandemonium, the voice in the trumpet was proceeding quite unperturbed.

"Silence!" shouted Bill, looking severely in the direction of the "seat of the scornful." "All please listen in on this. Mr. Meadowcroft is speaking." The confusion subsided and they heard these words:

" - sometimes impossible to get Mr. Edison's attention for weeks at a time. He has his meals brought in and sleeps in the laboratory - when he sleeps at all - and so intense is his interest in his work that it is useless to attempt to disturb him even for what seems to me to be business of the highest importance.

"But he has permitted me to express his deep and sincere interest in all you young people, and I am adding, on my own responsibility, three expressions of his which now seem to have maximum force because he has used them:

"'Never mind the milk that's spilt.'

"Genius is one per cent. *in*spiration, and ninety-nine per cent. *per*spiration.'

"'Don't watch - don't clock the watch - oh! - *don't* watch the CLOCK! - ' Why, Mr. Edison, I thought you - I have just been explaining why you couldn't come - and now (with a laugh) here you are!

"There was a hearty chuckle and another voice said:

"I know it's mean to make you a victim of misplaced confidence, but it came across me like a flash that I couldn't do a better thing for the Boy Scouts and Girls Scouts and all the 'good scouts,' old and young, than to broadcast a good word for my friend Marconi. So I have run up here to speak to the Radio Boys after all. I know it's a shame, but -"

"Nothing of the sort, Mr. Edison, - not on your life!" (It is the more familiar voice of Mr. Meadowcroft now.)

"Wait, let me introduce you: Boys and girls, you are now 'listening in' with Thomas Alva Edison, who said, like the young man in the parable, 'I go not,' then he changed his mind and went. He is here - not to give you any message for or about himself, but to express his regard for the man to whom all Radio Boys and Girls owe so much. Mr. Edison has come on purpose to say a word to you."

When the room was in a silence so solemn that those present could hear their own hearts beat, the voice the company now recognized as Mr. Edison's came through with trumpet clearness:

"I have great admiration and high regard for Marconi, the pioneer inventor of wireless communication. I wish you all the happiness that Comes through usefulness. Good night."

"Mr. Edison - one moment! In the name of the millions who are not 'listening in' on this, won't you please write this sentiment so that it can be seen as well as heard?"

"All right" - came through in Edison's voice. A brief pause ensued and - "Thank you, Mr. Edison," from Mr. Meadowcroft in a low tone, which he immediately raised:

"Mr. Edison has just written the words you have heard him speak to be broadcast, as it were, to the young eyes of America."[A]

Hearty cheers followed this closing announcement, but as the speakers they had heard were not aware of this, the demonstration soon ceased. Exuberant youth, however, must be heard, and so, led by the irrepressible Ted, they immediately sought fresh inspiration and began to cheer whomever and whatever came quickly into their minds; first Bill and Gus, with demands for a speech from Bill; then in answer to the school yell, they cheered the school and Professor Gray. Finally they began to cheer the refreshments as these suddenly developed a full-form materialization. But this was suddenly switched off into a sort of doubtful hurrah as Mr. Hooper, with his wife trying to dissuade him by his coat-tails, arose and cleared his throat.

"Lads and lasses: I sez to this 'ere lad, Bill Brown, sez I, some time back; I sez: 'Bill, me lad, if you ever fix it so's I kin hear my old friend Bill Medders talkin' out loud more'n a hunderd mile off,' I sez, 'then,' I sez, 'I'll give you a thousand dollers.' Well, this Bill, he sez: 'No, sir, Mr. Hooper,' he sez: 'We won't accept of no sich,' he sez, an' what he sez he sticks to, this 'ere lad Bill does, an' so does his buddy, Gus, 'ere. So, young people, I'm goin' to tell you what I'm a-goin' to do. I'm goin' to spend that thousand some way to sort o' remember this occasion by, an' it'll be spent fer whatever your teacher here an' Bill an' Gus an' any more that want to git into it sez it shall be. An', b'jinks, if you spring anything extry fine an' highfalutin I'll double it - make it two thousand; anything to help 'em along, gettin' an eddication, which I ain't got, ner never kin git, but my gal shall an' all her young friends. So, go to it, folks, an' I'm thinkin' my friends, Bill an' Gus -"

Roaring cheers interrupted the earnest speaker. He smiled broadly and sat down. Professor Gray got to his feet, but Bill, not seeing him, was first to be heard when the crowd silenced; the boy had got to the platform and then on a chair. Standing there balanced on his crutch, a hand where his shoulder usually rested, he was a sight to stir the pathos and inspire admiration in any crowd.

"I say, people, give three royal yells for Mr. Hooper! He's one of the dearest old chaps that ever drew breath! Ready, now -"

The roof didn't quite raise, but the nails may have been loosened some and the timbers strained. With the ceasing of the cheers, Bill shouted again:

"And now don't forget Professor Gray! He's going to be in on this deal, big, as you know!"

Again the walls trembled. Once more Bill was heard:

"And I have this suggestion: We'll put up a radio broadcasting station at the school. Get a government license, find means to make our service worth while and talk to anyone we want to. How's that?"

The building didn't crumble, but it surely shook. And then Professor Gray had the floor:

"Girls and boys, we mustn't forget William Brown and Augustus Grier. You can hardly mention one without the other. I propose -"

Gus shamelessly interrupted his respected teacher and friend:

"Three yells for Bill Brown's radio! Let her go!"

It went; as did also the refreshments a little later.

How Bill's idea of building a radio broadcasting station was carried out will be told in "Bill Brown Listens In."

# Choose from Thousands of 1stWorldLibrary Classics By

A. M. Barnard
Ada Leverson
Adolphus William Ward
Aesop
Agatha Christie
Alexander Aaronsohn
Alexander Kielland
Alexandre Dumas
Alfred Gatty
Alfred Ollivant
Alice Duer Miller
Alice Turner Curtis
Alice Dunbar
Allen Chapman
Ambrose Bierce
Amelia E. Barr
Amory H. Bradford
Andrew Lang
Andrew McFarland Davis
Andy Adams
Anna Alice Chapin
Anna Sewell
Annie Besant
Annie Hamilton Donnell
Annie Payson Call
Annie Roe Carr
Annonaymous
Anton Chekhov
Arnold Bennett
Arthur Conan Doyle
Arthur M. Winfield
Arthur Ransome
Arthur Schnitzler
Atticus
B.H. Baden-Powell
B. M. Bower
B. C. Chatterjee
Baroness Emmuska Orczy
Baroness Orczy
Basil King
Bayard Taylor
Ben Macomber
Bertha Muzzy Bower
Bjornstjerne Bjornson
Booth Tarkington
Boyd Cable
Bram Stoker
C. Collodi
C. E. Orr

C. M. Ingleby
Carolyn Wells
Catherine Parr Traill
Charles A. Eastman
Charles Amory Beach
Charles Dickens
Charles Dudley Warner
Charles Farrar Browne
Charles Ives
Charles Kingsley
Charles Klein
Charles Hanson Towne
Charles Lathrop Pack
Charles Romyn Dake
Charles Whibley
Charles Willing Beale
Charlotte M. Braeme
Charlotte M. Yonge
Charlotte Perkins Stetson
Clair W. Hayes
Clarence Day Jr.
Clarence E. Mulford
Clemence Housman
Confucius
Coningsby Dawson
Cornelis DeWitt Wilcox
Cyril Burleigh
D. H. Lawrence
Daniel Defoe
David Garnett
Dinah Craik
Don Carlos Janes
Donald Keyhoe
Dorothy Kilner
Dougan Clark
Douglas Fairbanks
E. Nesbit
E.P.Roe
E. Phillips Oppenheim
Earl Barnes
Edgar Rice Burroughs
Edith Van Dyne
Edith Wharton
Edward Everett Hale
Edward J. O'Biren
Edward S. Ellis
Edwin L. Arnold
Eleanor Atkins
Eliot Gregory

Elizabeth Gaskell
Elizabeth McCracken
Elizabeth Von Arnim
Ellem Key
Emerson Hough
Emilie F. Carlen
Emily Dickinson
Enid Bagnold
Enilor Macartney Lane
Erasmus W. Jones
Ernie Howard Pie
Ethel May Dell
Ethel Turner
Ethel Watts Mumford
Eugenie Foa
Eugene Wood
Eustace Hale Ball
Evelyn Everett-green
Everard Cotes
F. H. Cheley
F. J. Cross
F. Marion Crawford
Federick Austin Ogg
Ferdinand Ossendowski
Francis Bacon
Francis Darwin
Frances Hodgson Burnett
Frances Parkinson Keyes
Frank Gee Patchin
Frank Harris
Frank Jewett Mather
Frank L. Packard
Frank V. Webster
Frederic Stewart Isham
Frederick Trevor Hill
Frederick Winslow Taylor
Friedrich Kerst
Friedrich Nietzsche
Fyodor Dostoyevsky
G.A. Henty
G.K. Chesterton
Gabrielle E. Jackson
Garrett P. Serviss
Gaston Leroux
George A. Warren
George Ade
Geroge Bernard Shaw
George Durston
George Ebers

George Eliot
George Gissing
George MacDonald
George Meredith
George Orwell
George Sylvester Viereck
George Tucker
George W. Cable
George Wharton James
Gertrude Atherton
Gordon Casserly
Grace E. King
Grace Gallatin
Grace Greenwood
Grant Allen
Guillermo A. Sherwell
Gulielma Zollinger
Gustav Flaubert
H. A. Cody
H. B. Irving
H.C. Bailey
H. G. Wells
H. H. Munro
H. Irving Hancock
H. Rider Haggard
H. W. C. Davis
Haldeman Julius
Hall Caine
Hamilton Wright Mabie
Hans Christian Andersen
Harold Avery
Harold McGrath
Harriet Beecher Stowe
Harry Castlemon
Harry Coghill
Harry Houidini
Hayden Carruth
Helent Hunt Jackson
Helen Nicolay
Hendrik Conscience
Hendy David Thoreau
Henri Barbusse
Henrik Ibsen
Henry Adams
Henry Ford
Henry Frost
Henry James
Henry Jones Ford
Henry Seton Merriman
Henry W Longfellow
Herbert A. Giles

Herbert Carter
Herbert N. Casson
Herman Hesse
Hildegard G. Frey
Homer
Honore De Balzac
Horace B. Day
Horace Walpole
Horatio Alger Jr.
Howard Pyle
Howard R. Garis
Hugh Lofting
Hugh Walpole
Humphry Ward
Ian Maclaren
Inez Haynes Gillmore
Irving Bacheller
Isabel Hornibrook
Israel Abrahams
Ivan Turgenev
J.G.Austin
J. Henri Fabre
J. M. Barrie
J. Macdonald Oxley
J. S. Fletcher
J. S. Knowles
J. Storer Clouston
Jack London
Jacob Abbott
James Allen
James Andrews
James Baldwin
James Branch Cabell
James DeMille
James Joyce
James Lane Allen
James Lane Allen
James Oliver Curwood
James Oppenheim
James Otis
James R. Driscoll
Jane Austen
Jane L. Stewart
Janet Aldridge
Jens Peter Jacobsen
Jerome K. Jerome
John Burroughs
John Cournos
John F. Kennedy
John Gay
John Glasworthy

John Habberton
John Joy Bell
John Kendrick Bangs
John Milton
John Philip Sousa
Jonas Lauritz Idemil Lie
Jonathan Swift
Joseph A. Altsheler
Joseph Carey
Joseph Conrad
Joseph E. Badger Jr
Joseph Hergesheimer
Joseph Jacobs
Jules Vernes
Julian Hawthrone
Julie A Lippmann
Justin Huntly McCarthy
Kakuzo Okakura
Kenneth Grahame
Kenneth McGaffey
Kate Langley Bosher
Kate Langley Bosher
Katherine Cecil Thurston
Katherine Stokes
L. A. Abbot
L. T. Meade
L. Frank Baum
Latta Griswold
Laura Dent Crane
Laura Lee Hope
Laurence Housman
Lawrence Beasley
Leo Tolstoy
Leonid Andreyev
Lewis Carroll
Lewis Sperry Chafer
Lilian Bell
Lloyd Osbourne
Louis Hughes
Louis Tracy
Louisa May Alcott
Lucy Fitch Perkins
Lucy Maud Montgomery
Luther Benson
Lydia Miller Middleton
Lyndon Orr
M. Corvus
M. H. Adams
Margaret E. Sangster
Margret Howth
Margaret Vandercook

Margret Penrose
Maria Edgeworth
Maria Thompson Daviess
Mariano Azuela
Marion Polk Angellotti
Mark Overton
Mark Twain
Mary Austin
Mary Catherine Crowley
Mary Cole
Mary Hastings Bradley
Mary Roberts Rinehart
Mary Rowlandson
M. Wollstonecraft Shelley
Maud Lindsay
Max Beerbohm
Myra Kelly
Nathaniel Hawthrone
Nicolo Machiavelli
O. F. Walton
Oscar Wilde
Owen Johnson
P.G. Wodehouse
Paul and Mabel Thorne
Paul G. Tomlinson
Paul Severing
Percy Brebner
Peter B. Kyne
Plato
R. Derby Holmes
R. L. Stevenson
R. S. Ball
Rabindranath Tagore
Rahul Alvares
Ralph Bonehill
Ralph Henry Barbour
Ralph Victor
Ralph Waldo Emmerson
Rene Descartes
Rex Beach

Rex E. Beach
Richard Harding Davis
Richard Jefferies
Richard Le Gallienne
Robert Barr
Robert Frost
Robert Gordon Anderson
Robert L. Drake
Robert Lansing
Robert Lynd
Robert Michael Ballantyne
Robert W. Chambers
Rosa Nouchette Carey
Rudyard Kipling
Samuel B. Allison
Samuel Hopkins Adams
Sarah Bernhardt
Sarah C. Hallowell
Selma Lagerlof
Sherwood Anderson
Sigmund Freud
Standish O'Grady
Stanley Weyman
Stella Benson
Stella M. Francis
Stephen Crane
Stewart Edward White
Stijn Streuvels
Swami Abhedananda
Swami Parmananda
T. S. Ackland
T. S. Arthur
The Princess Der Ling
Thomas A. Janvier
Thomas A Kempis
Thomas Anderton
Thomas Bailey Aldrich
Thomas Bulfinch
Thomas De Quincey
Thomas Dixon

Thomas H. Huxley
Thomas Hardy
Thomas More
Thornton W. Burgess
U. S. Grant
Valentine Williams
Various Authors
Vaughan Kester
Victor Appleton
Victoria Cross
Virginia Woolf
Wadsworth Camp
Walter Camp
Walter Scott
Washington Irving
Wilbur Lawton
Wilkie Collins
Willa Cather
Willard F. Baker
William Dean Howells
William le Queux
W. Makepeace Thackeray
William W. Walter
William Shakespeare
Winston Churchill
Yei Theodora Ozaki
Yogi Ramacharaka
Young E. Allison
Zane Grey

www.ingramcontent.com/pod-product-compliance
Lightning Source LLC
Chambersburg PA
CBHW020505100426
42813CB00030B/3127/J